HOLLYWOOD MUSICALS

Hollywood Musicals offers an insightful account of a genre that was once a main-stay of twentieth-century film production and continues to draw audiences today.

What is a film musical? How do musicals work, formally and culturally? Why have they endured since the introduction of sound in the late 1920s? What makes them more than glittery surfaces or escapist fare? In answering such questions, this guidebook by Steven Cohan takes new and familiar viewers on a tour of Hollywood musicals. Chapters discuss definitions of the genre, its long history, different modes of analyzing it, the great stars of the classic era, and auteur directors. Highlights include extended discussions of such celebrated musicals from the studio era as *The Love Parade, Top Hat, Holiday Inn, Stormy Weather, The Gang's All Here, Meet Me in St. Louis, Cover Girl, Mother Wore Tights, Singin' in the Rain, Gentlemen Prefer Blondes, The Band Wagon, Seven Brides for Seven Brothers*, and *Jailhouse Rock* as well as later films, such as *Cabaret, All that Jazz, Beauty and the Beast*, and *La La Land*. Cohan brings in numerous other examples that amplify and extend to the present day his claims about the musical, its generic coherence and flexibility, its long and distinguished history, its special appeal, and its cultural significance.

Clear and accessible, this guide provides students of film and culture with a succinct but substantial overview that provides both analysis and intersectional context to one of Hollywood's most beloved genres.

Steven Cohan's books include *Masked Men: Masculinity and the Movies in the Fifties, Incongruous Entertainment: Camp, Cultural Value, and the MGM Musical*, and *Hollywood by Hollywood: The Backstudio Picture and the Mystique of Making Movies*. He is Dean's Distinguished Professor Emeritus at Syracuse University.

Routledge Film Guidebooks

The Routledge Film Guidebooks offer a clear introduction to and overview of the work of key filmmakers, movements or genres. Each guidebook contains an introduction, including a brief history; defining characteristics and major films; a chronology; key debates surrounding the filmmaker, movement or genre; and pivotal scenes, focusing on narrative structure, camera work and production quality.

For more information, visit: www.routledge.com/Routledge-Film-Guidebooks/book-series/SE0653

HOLLYWOOD MUSICALS

STEVEN COHAN

Routledge
Taylor & Francis Group

LONDON AND NEW YORK

First published 2020
by Routledge
2 Park Square, Milton Park, Abingdon, Oxon OX14 4RN

and by Routledge
52 Vanderbilt Avenue, New York, NY 10017

Routledge is an imprint of the Taylor & Francis Group, an informa business

British Library Cataloguing-in-Publication Data
A catalogue record for this book is available from the British Library

Library of Congress Cataloging-in-Publication Data
Names: Cohan, Steven, 1948– author.
Title: Hollywood musicals / Steven Cohan.
Description: London ; New York : Routledge, 2019. |
Series: Routledge film guidebooks | Includes bibliographical references and index. |
Identifiers: LCCN 2019024217 (print) | LCCN 2019024218 (ebook) |
ISBN 9781138497443 (hardback) | ISBN 9781138497450 (paperback) |
ISBN 9781351018746 (ebook)
Subjects: LCSH: Musical films–United States–History and criticism.
Classification: LCC PN1995.9.M86 C58 2019 (print) |
LCC PN1995.9.M86 (ebook) | DDC 791.43/750973–dc23
LC record available at https://lccn.loc.gov/2019024217
LC ebook record available at https://lccn.loc.gov/2019024218

ISBN: 978-1-138-49744-3 (hbk)
ISBN: 978-1-138-49745-0 (pbk)
ISBN: 978-1-351-01874-6 (ebk)

Typeset in Joanna MT Std
by Newgen Publishing UK

MIX
Paper from
responsible sources
FSC™ C013985

Printed in the United Kingdom
by Henry Ling Limited

For C.K.

CONTENTS

1

DEFINING THE MUSICAL

What exactly *is* a film musical? Many scholarly books on the musical begin with just this question, indicating that this genre is a slippery fish, indeed. At first the question may seem rhetorical, or at least an easy enough question to answer. Perhaps most everyone reading this book will instantly agree with Tom Brueggemann, writing for indiewire.com about "why musicals are box office gold again" with the release of *Mama Mia! Here We Go Again* (2018). He states, albeit parenthetically as if the genre is now strange enough that it needs defining for some contemporary readers, "(A musical is a film with singing actors, including numbers that aren't just stage performances)" (Brueggeman 2018). Fair enough as a starting point, but we need to amend his definition right away to include *dancing* actors along with *singing* ones. After all, some of the most important and influential stars of musicals during Hollywood's Golden Age—Fred Astaire, Eleanor Powell, Gene Kelly—were known for their dancing, which they choreographed themselves.

More important, though: why does Brueggeman privilege "numbers that aren't just stage performances"? No doubt he has in mind those numbers in which, like the soliloquies in Shakespeare's plays, characters spontaneously express their innermost feelings or thoughts, whether through a song or a dance or both, and whether as a solo or duet, or with a full ensemble. Certainly, many musicals feature such musical moments to reveal a character's desire, joy, conflict, sadness, or insecurity. By the same token, the convention of having characters burst into song, their vocalizing accompanied by an unseen orchestra that does not exist in the fictional world, may occasion laughter or even discomfort from today's audiences due to its breaking with codes of cinematic realism. Indeed, to work around that convention of suddenly breaking into song for twenty-first-century viewers, *Chicago* (2002) framed almost each number as fantasies of the heroine, Roxie Hart (Renée Zellwegger), thereby creating the impression that the film's musical moments were happening in her mind.

Yet there are also scores of musicals that feature only show numbers taking place in the fictional world (or the "diegesis") on a theater stage or in a night club, as a film within a film, or offstage but with onscreen accompaniment from a record player or the radio. Betty Grable's hugely popular backstage musicals of the 1940s tend to be of this type. A good example is *Coney Island* (1943). Grable performs eight stage numbers and a ninth with costar George Montgomery when they join a group of picnickers singing the title tune to their own musical accompaniment. Similarly, in *A Star Is Born* (1954), all but one of Judy Garland's numbers take place on stage, in a jazz club, on a sound stage, in a recording studio, as a film within a film, or in her character's home with a rehearsal record playing on the phonograph. Biopics about real-life performers, such as *The Jolson Story* (1946) about Al Jolson and *Lady Sings the Blues* (1968) about Billy Holliday, feature mainly stage performances, too. *Woodstock* (1970), chronicling the famous music festival of 1969, and *The Last Waltz* (1978), recounting The Band's farewell concert in 1976, also have many musical numbers that are filmed stage performances. Although concert films such as those two tend to be classified as documentaries, many scholars consider them to be musicals as well.

What Brueggemann's definition further sidesteps are musicals in which characters never sing. I have in mind dance musicals such as *Saturday Night Fever* (1977) and *Flashdance* (1983). Variants are ballet films such as Gene Kelly's *Invitation to the Dance* (1956), composed entirely of three long dance sequences. For that matter, some of the earliest examples of the genre following the introduction of sound, such as *Hollywood Revue of 1929* (1929) and *The Show of Shows* (1929), have singing and dancing but lack a plot with characters as they are filmed revues. Revues were a staple of Broadway during the first part of the twentieth century; in the 1950s they moved to television as variety shows. Lacking a storyline, filmed revues of this early moment in the history of sound were all-star affairs comprised of many different styled numbers interspersed with comedic sketches, and they were meant to show off both the new sound technology and a studio's stable of new and old contract players, speaking, singing, or dancing for the first time on screen.

Most musicals, however, do thread numbers through a plot that creates characters for the actors to play. When revues were briefly revived during wartime in the 1940s, most added a thin backstage storyline to give the semblance of a narrative holding the film together. However formulaic or silly, the plot at least enables an audience to catch its breath, so to speak, in between numbers, which tend to create a different kind of effect on viewers due to the energy of dancing, the intensity of singing, or the spectacle of a big production number. Todd Decker argues that Fred Astaire's dancing is "always the primary reason for his films; the plot remains secondary, a necessary 'hanger' for the musical numbers" (Decker 2011, 25). Even though numbers are a musical's singular attraction, however, distinguishing it from other genres, and while one does not watch musicals for their plots alone, the importance of narrative cannot be underestimated. The relation between numbers and narrative is a useful way to begin thinking further about how musicals work as a genre.

Writing on Busby Berkeley's output, Martin Rubin calls the musical "an impossible genre," which is to say that at least some numbers are "impossible—that is, impossible from the standpoint of the realistic discourse of the narrative" (Rubin 1993, 37). For instance, the sole number in *A Star Is Born* without an onscreen source for the music has to cheat a bit, indicating its "impossibility." Judy Garland's voice is initially heard on a radio playing a recording of "It's a New World." After James Mason turns the device off so she can sing the song to him directly, Garland sings the verse acapella, but an off-screen orchestra soon accompanies her when she begins the chorus. This example, however, may also be a bit misleading for Rubin is not simply referring, as Brueggeman is, to "numbers that aren't stage performances," but instead argues that a musical features numbers that are impossible *spatially* as well as *narratively* regardless of where they happen in the narrative. For in addition to the "impossibility" of characters breaking into song or dancing in the street, Rubin argues, even backstage musicals

> establish a space (or a series of homologous spaces) that are, to a cer-
> tain extent, self-enclosed and independent of the surrounding narrative.
> This renders the space accessible to spectacular expansions and
> distortions that can be clearly in excess of the narrative without neces-
> sarily disrupting it.
>
> (36)

Given the long-standing protocols of continuity editing, effaced camera work, and a high degree of mimetic illusionism that dominate mainstream cinema, a film musical cannot easily dispense with conventions of realism altogether, whereas on stage in a real theater a musical can be evocative and abstract in its set designs, configuration of actors in multiple spaces on the stage, and even the narrative continuity of the book (the term for the libretto of a stage musical). Yet on film even when the singing and dancing in numbers may be happening in the realistic world of the story and, as in backstage musicals, are recognized in the fictional world *as* a stage performance for a diegetic audience, the numbers' treatment as filmed and edited usually does something "impossible" to the narrative's otherwise more realistic sense of cinematic space.

As Rubin points out, Berkeley's numbers are impossible in terms of their scale, moving onto enormous soundstages that dispel the illusion they are happening on the theatrical stage where they are supposedly taking place; and in terms of their effects, made possible only via camera work, editing, and the special effects lab (Rubin 1993: 38–39). Show numbers in Berkeley's *Gold Diggers of 1933* (1933), for instance, begin on a realistically defined stage but quickly transform this "stage" into a vast space that no theater could possibly contain, both in terms of *where* the number is happening and, with the famous Berkeleyesque overhead shots that form abstract visual patterns out of the showgirls, *from where* the number could conceivably be viewed.

To provide a specific example from *Gold Diggers of 1933*, "The Shadow Waltz" opens with a shot of the orchestra and first rows of the audience facing the stage as the curtain rises. Dick Powell walks out and sings to Ruby Keeler. As he finishes, a quartet of ghostly chorines sing, their faded figures initially superimposed onto the frame behind the two stars. The camera then moves back to show Powell playing the violin as Keeler dances; he embraces her as she joins him in singing to conclude this first sequence. So far, the editing showcases the two star performers and respects the spatial limitations of a Broadway stage, where the number is happening diegetically according to the narrative; even the ghostly quartet could have been achieved onstage in a real playhouse with a scrim and changes of lighting.

However, when the duo finish, Berkeley cuts to a more fantastic, surreal setting that can only be rendered as cinema, not on a theater's proscenium stage. Sixty showgirls, costumed in glittery gowns with triple gyrating hoop skirts, sing and play violins on a multileveled circular set. Each cut reveals more of the expansive space in which their movement occurs. The image suddenly darkens and only the electrified violins are illuminated. Incongruously, with an equally abrupt restoration of full lighting, an overhead shot of the women circling around

Figure 1.1 In "The Shadow Waltz" from *Gold Diggers of 1933* (1933, Warner Bros.) showgirls twirl and play violins

a single twirling figure makes them look like a flower opening and closing. Another overhead shot then shows only neon violins again in darkness; the chorines break their circular configuration to form a giant violin out of their smaller illuminated instruments, with a huge neon bow coming from who knows where. An abrupt shift to a reflective pool shows the ensemble one after another with their skirts held high and legs exposed, then the camera tilts and shows dancing chorines opposite their reflections, and the women and their mirror images appear sideways in two columns on the screen. The camera pans across another row of chorines singing and looking at their watery reflections, and the number ends with a closeup of Powell and Keeler in a clinch, as a rose falls into the water.

"The Shadow Waltz" is impossible because it does not adhere to a realistic sense of space given the number's ostensible setting in the

Figure 1.2 An overhead shot in "The Shadow Waltz" turns these human figures into an image that evokes a flower opening and closing

fiction on a theater's proscenium stage. Once Powell and Keeler conclude the opening segment, Berkeley's filming disaggregates what we see onscreen from what the onscreen audience, limited by the perspective of their seats in the theater, could possibly be watching in story time. Not all stage numbers are as fantastic as Berkeley's, of course, but his musicals well exemplify how the impossible space of a number is, in a word, *cinematic* (that is, viewable and hence experienced only through the apparatus of the cinema) rather than realistic in the sense of being "true to life" and limited to a single human perspective. Despite how Hollywood's codes of realism have always worked to efface the apparatus of cinema through continuity editing respective of a single viewing position, here instead of being the proverbial window affording access to a fictional world, the camera—by virtue of its motion, its position, and the editing—is in effect seeing for the spectator.

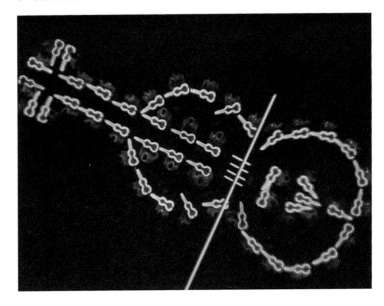

Figure 1.3 Another overhead shot in "The Shadow Waltz" transforms the women into a neon violin

Impossible numbers do not happen only on an imaginary stage, as happens in Berkeley's musicals. Furthermore, a number's impossibility can be achieved even when filming outside of a studio soundstage or backlot, where all elements can be controlled, and even when the editing assures a sense of realistic continuity. The musical's impossibility as a genre, in short, exists on a continuum with the kind of effects Berkeley achieved at one extreme and more subtle legerdemain, as in *A Star Is Born* where the numbers do not noticeably disrupt the narrative's illusionism, at the other extreme.

Consider, for instance, the opening of Robert Wise's *The Sound of Music* (1965). For two and a half minutes, edited overhead shots identify the Austrian setting: an aerial camera slowly moves downward in space from the snow-covered Alps, with the noise of strong, harsh winds on the soundtrack, to a glimpse of the countryside's lush greenery and waterways in the distance, as birds chirp in the background. Once we see a river and trees in the foreground, the birds' singing becomes more musical as wind instruments start to play along; the aerial camera now tours the countryside as horns join the woodwinds to sound the first notes of the title song. The camera nears ground level at a grassy clearing and, the orchestra beginning to swell, we finally see a human figure approaching from the far distance. As Julie Andrews, playing the novitiate Maria, reaches the foreground, she twirls and begins to sing a few notes of "The Sound of Music." With a cut to a medium shot of her, Andrews sings the song in earnest.

"The Sound of Music" recounts Maria's appreciation of and affinity with nature through her vocalizing. "The hills are alive," she sings, "… with songs they have sung for a thousand years." Her song indicates how the musicality of nature, as voiced by her singing, gives her a sense of liberation, a respite from the confinement of the convent to which she will soon return. As filmed and edited under Wise's direction, the number expresses the joy Maria feels, and it does so through its expansive filming of space, beginning with the aerial camerawork, which frames the number cinematically. For not only is Maria singing with Julie Andrews's obviously trained voice to an unseen orchestra but, when she sings of trees there is a cut to her walking through a tree-lined area; when she sings of a brook, another cut shows her walking along water; to finish the song, the editing rhymes with the number's opening, as she runs up the grassy hillside to sing about going to the hills when she feels lonely. Then a cut to another medium shot isolates her body from those hills by depicting her against a blue-gray sky, foregrounding Andrews as the picture's star. At this point the sound of church bells in the diegesis are heard, breaking the number's "impossible" spell. With the camera and star both grounded at the number's end, her character realizes she is late and has to rush back to the convent, first racing away from the camera, then returning to retrieve her forgotten hat. The orchestra disappears from the soundtrack and we hear Maria's nonsinging voice for the first time when she shouts, "Oh!" as she picks up the hat and rushes back from where she came.

Figure 1.4 Julie Andrews in *The Sound of Music* (1965, Twentieth Century-Fox)

What the camera observes in this sequence, more constrained than in a Berkeley musical, nonetheless renders the number's impossibility because, in its expansive sense of natural space, it visualizes how singing liberates Maria and her body from more earthbound concerns while associating her single figure with the lush natural environment. Subsequently in *The Sound of Music*, Maria's impossible, full-voiced, and rhyming spontaneous expression in the opening becomes a bona fide and thus a very possible song when the Von Trapp children sing it acapella for the Baroness (Eleanor Parker). What is more, their father (Christopher Plummer) apparently knows the words, too, as he (along with a full orchestra) joins in the singing.

For the most part, how numbers are shot and edited, their singing, tapping, and sound effects recorded, further emphasize a musical's impossibility. Actors in narrative sequences rarely face the camera directly, first so that their gaze implies realistic dimensions of narrative space (somewhat modeled on perspective in Renaissance painting) and second so that it encourages a viewer's identification with the performer as a character. In musical numbers, by contrast, performers tend to face the camera—and hence the moviegoing audience—more directly. By changing registers in the film's narrative, such a turn from indirect to direct address produces an impression of watching a "live" performance because it shifts attention from character to performer, from Maria to Julie Andrews. In this respect a viewer may experience a doubled or split identification while watching a number, identifying with the character in the narrative all the while standing outside the narrative momentarily to respond to the power of the singer's perform-ance (Feuer 1993: 36). When I saw *Funny Girl* (1968) during its prem-iere roadshow run in Los Angeles, the audience applauded after each of Barbra Streisand's numbers, momentarily rupturing their identifica-tion with her characterization of Fanny Brice in the narrative. Likewise, the more recent phenomenon of singing along to the numbers in *The Sound of Music* reflects an audience's momentary disengagement from the narrative and reengagement with the film through collectively identi-fying with Andrews's performance by enacting it along with her.

The protocols for producing musical numbers, refined during the early 1930s and still continuing for the most part today, assure a "perfect" performance, vocally and visually, while also enhancing the number's "impossibility," which is to say that a number is always more than a simple recording of a "live" performance happening before a camera. Like narrative sequences in musicals and nonmusicals alike, moreover, numbers are edited from multiple takes. "The Sound of Music," for example, was comprised out of multiple shots, each requiring different setups and not necessarily all filmed on the same day, with the continuity of Andrews's singing giving a sonic unity and sense of her embodied presence to the entire sequence despite shifts in its editing. Andrews's singing was prerecorded before filming, which is why her spoken "Oh" when she retrieves the hat marks a subtle shift in registers from her doing a star turn in the number to her performing as a character, Maria, in the narrative.

The first musicals in the late 1920s and early 1930s recorded singing live with an orchestra playing out of camera range, a microphone concealed somewhere on set, and the camera confined to a vault-like glass booth, known as the "icebox," for soundproofing, which kept it pretty fixed to a single position (McBride 2018: 234). *Singin' in the Rain* uses some of that old equipment when representing the making of early talkies. Obviously, it was a cumbersome process, especially difficult when it came to making a musical. Another practice quickly replaced it by 1930. The singing, accompanied by a full orchestra, was prerecorded in a studio's recording studio, creating a playback disk for filming. Gerald Mast describes the advantages of this new protocol, which became the industry standard:

> The method has obvious advantages of both sound and sight. The quality of the sound recording and the vocal performance can be controlled and assured in advance. Filming on the set can then be much freer, concentrating exclusively on a visual interpretation of the number and a projection of its musical energy into visual space. The film director enjoyed considerable freedom to play with visual imagery, divorcing its strict synchronization to vocalized lyrics, which could carry on without visual aid. A film could juxtapose any arresting, ironic, evocative, or clever visual image with the continuity of prerecorded music.
>
> (Mast 1987: 92)

If the performer was not a strong singer, the record might be comprised from several takes or a vocal double was used. Great dancers like Rita Hayworth, Cyd Charisse, and Vera-Ellen were routinely dubbed in their musicals, with professional singers preparing the prerecordings of their numbers. So too were some actors who lacked enough training or could not hold a tune. Bill Lee, for example, was Plummer's voice double when Baron Von Trapp joins his children in singing "The Sound of Music." Marnie Nixon was Audrey Hepburn's singing voice for *My Fair Lady* (1964), although Hepburn herself sang all her numbers in *Funny Face* (1957). During the number's filming, the star would lip-synch or mime the lyrics, or she might sing as the prerecording was played back but her voice would not be recorded. Judy Garland was known for singing on set so loudly when performing a number before the camera that she would drown out her own playback, but the voice subsequently wedded to her image for the release print was her singing as recorded at another time and in another space at the studio. Along with other sound effects for a number, the sounds of tapping feet were then postrecorded, sometimes months after filming and frequently by someone other than the dancer, who may have been working on another film. Hermes Pan, for instance, postrecorded Ginger Rogers's taps for the series of musicals she starred in with Fred Astaire at RKO during the 1930s, whereas Astaire postrecorded his own.

Finally, often in the release print the singing usually and noticeably differed in volume, echo, and reverberation from the spoken dialogue leading up to it; this was due to differences in how and where singing and speaking were each recorded. Due to the limits of studio-era technology, in the music studio, as opposed to dialogue filmed on set, singing could be recorded with the microphone closer to the body. As a result, Alan Williams has noted, "The space of the musical number becomes *larger* than the space of the narrative," with this impression of expansion occurring "as the distortion (but not destruction) of an initially coherent space" (Williams 1981:149, his emphasis). Prerecording technology enhanced the impossibility of numbers because singing on screen differed from dialogue in its sound but also in terms of how the former "conveys a sense of relative *spacelessness*" (151, his emphasis). Although monaural playback in standard movie theaters differed from the new stereophonic speakers of the 1950s in downtown and other luxury movie palaces, to be sure, this distinction pretty much held true for most classic era musicals.

As Jennifer Fleeger points out, the filmed body in every genre appears to unite the separate registers of sound and image so that the voice appears to emanate directly from that body. However, she goes on to claim, "a *musical* body performs a double deception: the illusion of wholeness generated by the singing body and the perceived unity of the piece he [or she] performs remove the spectator's attention even further from the process of production" (Fleeger 2014: 21). Much of this "double deception" results from how the editing and prominence of the performer in the frame can smooth over the possibility of rupturing the cinematic illusion of an authentic and embodied presence that the practices of pre- and postrecording may otherwise appear to cause. The postmodern musical, *Pennies from Heaven* (1981), produces its Brechtian effect of alienation on the part of viewers because the performers—Steve Martin, Bernadette Peters, and others—do not sing in their own voices but mime to recordings from the 1930s. That they open their mouths and, like the cat that swallowed the canary in a cartoon, out comes Bing Crosby's voice or Helen Kane's or the Boswell Sisters, often without regard for the character's gender, makes vivid the disaggregation of what we see from what we hear. The disorienting effect here is achieved because it goes against the grain of over five prior decades of musicals working hard if invisibly to unite the voice with the filmed body. By contrast, recent musicals like *Les Miserables* (2012) have claimed in their promotion that numbers have been recorded "live," usually to the score played on piano and heard via a tiny earpiece, to emphasize the performers' authenticity, but even then editing of this recorded performance, the subsequent addition of orchestral accompaniment, and probable enhancement of some voices by autotuning come into play afterward.

Numbers are obviously central to understanding how musicals work. Regardless of whether they happen onscreen as stage performances or as spontaneous expressions of a character's emotions, numbers are not only a distinguishing feature of the genre but central to appreciating a given film's simplicity or its complexity in musical terms. When a performer, Judy Garland, Julie Andrews, or Barbra Streisand, say, sings onscreen, the moment is thrilling because it embodies a liberating sensibility, one transcendent of the limitations of ordinary life with its problems, worries, conflicts, and disappointments. Whereas singing locates such feelings in the voice and the face, with hands and posture in support, dancing inscribes them on the entire body. It makes perfect sense for a great dancer like Fred Astaire to dance on the ceiling in *Royal Wedding* (1950) or on clouds in *The Belle of New York* (1951) because dancing enables his lithe figure to embody a sense of being lighter than air, even when he is tapping on the floor. Astaire does not need special effects to resist gravity, moreover. He can simply walk, his body's musicality liberating him from being grounded like other earthlings.

Figure 1.5 Fred Astaire in *Royal Wedding* (1951, MGM)

Easter Parade (1948) begins with Astaire strolling down the street, raising his hat, bowing his head when greeting people as he passes, singing "Happy Easter" to them. The sequence starts with him in a full body shot as he whistles to the melody of "Happy Easter," one hand to his vest, the other jauntily brandishing a walking stick. As he approaches the camera, his position shifts to a medium shot as the camera follows him. In walking, Astaire moves his entire body as if he is about to go into a dance; he first secures the walking stick under one arm and places his hands behind his back; then he turns around to look at a store window; coming back full circle, he twirls and spins the walking stick. Waving it, he enters the fashion salon where the song "Happy Easter" is passed on to the floor models. This opening establishes the musicality of Astaire's body in contrast with the various strangers he greets on the street. For Astaire walking is an inchoate form of dancing; even his pedestrian motion here signifies

Figure 1.6 Fred Astaire in *Easter Parade* (1948, MGM)

his boundless energy, innate sense of rhythm, and physical eloquence as a dancer.

Astaire is a singular performer whose movement onscreen appears effortlessly to resonate as physical liberation through the musicality of his body. The affective pleasure of watching a performer's musicality onscreen is one of the great pleasures that musical films have traditionally offered spectators. As the classical musical ceased to be produced with any degree of regularity, many music videos used dance to connote this sense of embodied freedom regardless of the narrative hook or song's content. In "Billy Jean" (1983), to give an example, Michael Jackson's movement alternates between walking and dancing to the point where one becomes the other.

The same sense of embodied liberation through choreographed movement characterizes the action film as well; in fact, scholars tend to refer to the big sequences featuring stunts, explosions, and stylized violence as "numbers," suggesting how their lineage indirectly refers back to production numbers in musicals. Action numbers are as costly and time-consuming as production numbers were, and, like dance numbers, they also can foreground the performer's physical eloquence through stunt work, as in Hong Kong cinema. Action numbers likewise achieve something akin to the musical's double-deception, its "impossibility," as the action hero's body, often a composite of the star and various stunt doubles, works to embody the illusion of physical unity onscreen while the number's visceral effect, its "wow" factor due to fights, explosions, or car chases, distracts the viewer's attention from the complex means of production.

Action numbers remind us that the "impossible" pleasures formally associated with musicals now reverberate through other genres, too. Edgar Wright, who wrote and directed *Baby Driver* (2017), states that his crime caper film "is not just an action film. It's more like an action musical. ... The key is actually not that it is edited to the music, but more crucially it's choreographed to the music" (Burlingame 2018). Narratively, the musical soundtrack reflects Baby's (Ansel Egort) reliance on music to block out the whining sound of tinnitus in his ears. The opening sequence is a bravura action number comprising many stunt drivers as wheelman Baby expertly steers the getaway car all over Atlanta following a bank robbery. But what drew most attention in all quarters—reviewers, viewers, and the technical awards circuit—after the film premiered in multiplexes was the "choreography" Wright spoke of: the background noise—wailing sirens, barking dogs, car revs, horns, and so on—is edited to be "in sympathy" to the beat of the music pounding in Baby's ears, creating the impression that "the world around him dances to the same beat" (Trenholm 2018).

Even more to the point, *Baby Driver* may not be a musical, but Ansel Egort moves like a character in one. While waiting in the getaway car, Baby lip-synchs to the singing on his ear phones, pounds and beats on the steering wheel, flashes the wipers, slaps his head, smacks his hand on the car door, twists his head, plays air guitar, all perfectly timed to the beat of "Bellbottoms" by the John Spenser Blues Explosion. Egort is miming what could be a musical performance in a musical. Following the chase and during the main titles, Baby goes to fetch coffee for the gang; as he strides to the rhythm of the music, Bob & Earl's "Harlem Shuffle," he dances along the downtown streets. Baby moves his head and arms, sways his torso, shakes his shoulders, shimmies around a streetlamp, plays an air trumpet. His choreographed high-stepping is directly responsive to what he and we hear on the soundtrack. The singers chant, "You move to the right," and Baby does just that, posing in profile in front of a store window. Even when plainly walking he does so rhythmically, much as Astaire does in *Easter Parade* and Jackson in "Billie Jean." As Wright explained, when filming *Baby Driver* "everything was so precise that the actors understood this was like a musical" (Burlingame 2018).

Baby Driver is a "musical action film," the soundtrack beats in sympathetic rapport with the action, and Egort jives to the music his character hears, his performance physically embodying the music much as Astaire and Jackson did when they danced, so why can't *Baby Driver* be considered a musical? Although the onscreen action is choreographed to the soundtrack, the soundtrack serves to reinforce the action, becoming more subordinate as narrative complications about the heist and the gang's mistrust of each other accumulate. *Baby Driver* evokes the pleasures of a traditional musical while using this evocation to serve

Figure 1.7 Ansel Egort in *Baby Driver* (2017, TriStar Pictures)

a different genre. It is not a musical though it helps one to appreciate what musicals do when they foreground a performer's onscreen embodiment of musicality, whether as a singer or dancer, and how a surrounding narrative functions in relation to numbers.

In formal terms, musicals use narrative as a frame on which to hang numbers, as I have previously noted, which is also to say that numbers punctuate and pace the narrative. Two stylistic logics have dominated the musical throughout its history: the logic of an *integrated* form and aesthetic and that of an *aggregated* form and aesthetic. An integrated musical gives the impression that numbers move the narrative along, whether because they deepen a sense of characters' motives and feelings or because they effect transitions from one action to the next, from one scene to the next. In Vincente Minnelli's *Meet Me in St. Louis* (1944), for instance, which some scholars consider the perfect expression of the genre's integrated style, the numbers happen as outgrowths of the narrative, deepening a sense of character development for Judy Garland, defining the family's coherence as an emotional entity, and furthering or complicating the action; for that matter, given the style, the Halloween sequence featuring the children, which is not a number, can seem to function as one. An integrated musical like this one makes the transition from narrative to number and back again stylistically fluid so that narrative scenes could become numbers at any moment. This effect is often achieved (1) through musical underscoring, which anticipates the melody of a song, (2) when the orchestration or dialogue increases in volume as part of the pre-recording to introduce the number, and (3) because in his or her stance and delivery the performer seems able to turn dialogue into a song or a bodily gesture into a dance move at the slightest inclination, as when Astaire's gait already expresses his musicality before a number begins.

The aggregated musical, best typified by backstage musicals such as Busby Berkeley's or those at Twentieth Century-Fox starring Betty Grable or Alice Faye, stylistically brackets numbers from the narrative. This is why most (but not all) aggregated musicals are backstage narratives. In contrast with the integrated musical, an aggregated musical seems to add one number after another primarily as a distraction from the narrative because numbers momentarily pause the action, as happens with the inclusion of Big Band numbers in so many musicals of the 1940s. Berkeley's 1930s musicals tend to stack several numbers, one after the other, and for musicals like *Gold Diggers of 1933* he directed the numbers while someone else, in this case Mervyn LeRoy, directed the narrative sections, indicating the paralleled but distinctive realms of number and narrative in this film. Show numbers can be easily bracketed off from the narrative because they occur in a different fictional space such as a theater stage, they usually have more stylized sets and costumes, they oftentimes use different performers to partner a star and feature specialty acts momentarily to occupy the spotlight, and they are filmed and edited differently than narrative scenes.

Many numbers in an aggregated musical could conceivably be shuffled and reordered or even deleted (as some numbers were during post-production or after previews) without harming the narrative. Eight of the numbers featuring Betty Grable singing and dancing in *Coney Island*, as noted already, occur on a stage while George Montgomery and Cesar Romero, who do not perform with her, try to outmaneuver the other to run the nightspot in Coney Island. In pausing the narrative, the accumulation of Grable's numbers is by no means irrelevant. In musicals like this one, which pair a singing actress and a nonsinging actor, Susan Smith points out, "the resulting imbalance in their relationship often tends to provoke a more traumatic set of gender-related tensions and anxieties" (Smith 2005: 79). This imbalance should be understood in formal and musical as well as ideological terms, because while in its story the male figure may bear the weight of patriarchal superiority over the female, she has all the numbers, which in this genre gives her the greater claim to our attention.

Thus in *Coney Island* Grable's numbers do not bear directly on Montgomery and Romero's rivalry, which drives the narrative and treats her character like a pawn passed back and forth between them, but the numbers do recount changes in Grable's performance style as her character becomes a star and moves from Romero's night club in the amusement park to the legitimate stage. As important to the aggregative style of *Coney Island*, the incremental placement of numbers paces its narrative trajectory, establishing a formal rhythm for the musical. Thus two parallel interests organize *Coney Island*: the men's narrative and Grable's increasingly lavish numbers, which are the film's main attraction since the narrative is a pretty standard one for Fox. Indeed, that the film's narrative is detachable from its numbers accounts for how Fox could remake *Coney Island* as *Wabash Avenue* (1950) seven years later, using Grable and the same plot but with different actors and different numbers.

There can also be hybrids of the two forms. No doubt because it is a backstager, while *Easter Parade* follows an integrative aesthetic in its visual and aural styles, so that Astaire and costar Judy Garland seesaw effortlessly and seamlessly between narrative scenes and numbers, many of this film's fifteen numbers are show numbers that advance the narrative mainly as signposts marking the stars' emergence as a successful stage team. This is the sense in which Decker noted that plot in an Astaire musical is there simply to hang the numbers together, which is another way to describe an aggregated aesthetic. Only a few numbers happen off stage as spontaneous expressions of powerful feelings, but the integrated aesthetic, which dominates the visual and aural style of *Easter Parade*, makes believable these musical moments when characters burst into song and dance (as in Astaire's opening two numbers, "Happy Easter" and "Drum Crazy," his duet with Ann Miller, "It Only Happens When I Dance with You," Garland's and Peter Lawford's duet in the street, "A Fella with an Umbrella," and her closing two numbers, "Better Luck Next Time" and "Easter Parade"). Stylistically, there is not much difference in the handling of these numbers, which happen off stage in the narrative, and that of the numbers happening on a stage or in a nightclub.

One can, in fact, watch just the numbers of *Easter Parade* to get a sense of narrative progression from some (such as the numbers explicitly charting the evolution of Astaire's discovery of how best to team with Garland, climaxing in their hobo turn in "A Couple of Swells," and their simultaneously falling in love), indicating the pull of integration on the film, while noticing those numbers that stall the narrative despite being great musical performances (such as Astaire's two opening numbers, his "Steppin' Out with My Baby," or Ann Miller's two big production numbers), indicating the pull of aggregation. One number epitomizing the hybrid form of *Easter Parade* are the two reprises of "It Only Happens When I Dance with You." Astaire first sings this song spontaneously as an expression of his feelings for Miller yet when Garland later sings it while rehearsing with Astaire, and he and Miller dance to it after his and Garland's big opening night, the number has become a show tune in the diegesis.

Regardless of their aggregated, integrated, or hybrid form, musicals are, well, expressly about *music*, which is another reason why *Baby Driver* may borrow tropes from the musical without becoming one. Obviously, music is a musical's *raison d'être*; whether the songs are great, serviceable for their purposes, or mediocre, they are why one watches a musical as opposed to turning to another genre. Another indication of music's centrality can be found in the frequency with which songs self-reflexively refer to "singing," "song," "dance," "dancing," or "music" in their titles or lyrics. According to Jane Feuer, musicals use this convention to define music as American popular songs, identifying them as a "lyrical extension" of ordinary speech, as when spoken dialogue leads into the verse of a song, while also affiliating this music with a vernacular and non-European style, namely jazz as loosely understood in the first half of the twentieth century (Feuer 1993: 53).

One other indication of music's importance is how often musicals make it a central theme organizing their narrative. In nonbackstage musicals the thematic value of music may appear indirectly, as when songs identity the Smiths' unity as a family through music and songs resolve the conflict over their having to move to New York City in *Meet Me in St. Louis* (see Chapter 3). In backstage musicals, music more openly drives the narrative of putting on a show, and the show is inevitably … wait for it … a musical! Whether integrated or aggregated in their form, backstage musicals give characters ample and plausible reasons to go into a song or dance. Inevitably, too, the show's success and the formation of the main romantic couple are equated. Either the couple's resolution of their conflicts helps to solve the problems of a troubled production, or the production's triumph somehow brings the right couple back together before the end titles, as happens in *Coney Island*.

The sheer number of backstage musicals, in fact, ought to make one wonder why the genre keeps turning to theater and not to film. Yes, what has become the justifiably most celebrated backstage musical, *Singin' in the Rain*, is about filmmaking and not theater, but it stands out as the proverbial exception that proves the rule. Jane Feuer argues that backstage musicals work to demystify the processes of producing entertainment only to be "followed by a new mystification, the celebration of the seamless final show or placing back on her pedestal of a disgraced performer" (Feuer 1993: 44). The "final show" is usually a big production number, or sequence of numbers, that celebrates popular entertainment by taking full advantage of filmmaking. In using theater as their backdrop, backstage musicals demystify live entertainment in order to remystify it as *cinema*, the film we are watching.

However, it does not follow that the film musical owes no debts to the stage since the two media—cinema and live theatre—have historically cross-fertilized each other, starting with film adaptations of Broadway hits and, in this century, Broadway's musicalized versions of well-known films like *An American in Paris* (1951; on Broadway 2015–2016). Historically, vaudeville led to the backstage musical; typically, the show being put on looks like a revue with all sorts of numbers by the film's stars, supporting players, and specialty acts (even though oftentimes there may be dialogue about the show having a plot). This is why backstage musicals tend to be the most aggregated in their form.

In his structuralist anatomy of the musical Rick Altman in *The American Film Musical* (1989) calls this subgenre the *show musical*. By comparison, early musical comedies on the legitimate stage derived in part from the European operetta, which led to what Altman terms the *fairy tale musical*. The operetta and early musical comedies both tended to work their plots around two pairs of characters, a romantic couple and a comic one. The Astaire-Rodgers musicals, all fairy tale musicals according to Altman, follow this format with the two stars alternating between playing the romantic duo opposite older supporting players (*Top Hat* (1935) and *Swing Time* (1936) and playing the comic duo opposite costars their same age (*Roberta* (1935) and *Follow the Fleet* (1936)). A third subgenre in Altman's schema is the folk musical such as *Meet Me in St. Louis*. The principle of ameliorating unity in the show musical is the show, in the fairy tale musical it is the couple, and in the folk musical it is the community. Show musicals tend to focus on the boundaries between and parallels of real life and the stage, whereas fairy tale musicals enact the couple's mutual sexual attraction despite their differences and the folk musical locates the community in a premodern period of American history. Desirée Garcia convincingly argues, moreover, that the folk musical, which was most popular in the 1940s during and for several years after World War II, celebrates "a collective rooted in mythic space and time before the dislocation and alienation of the modern era fundamentally altered relationships to people and to homeland" (Garcia 2014: 5). The folk musical, she shows, derives from ethnic and race musicals of the 1930s, like the Yiddish and all-black musicals produced outside of Hollywood.

To return to the question that opened this chapter: what is a musical? Scholars of the musical like Sean Griffin and Barry Keith Grant agree that musicals are about performing music, singing, and/or dancing, and I have been working from this definition as well (Grant 2012: 1; Griffin 2018: 3). The genre may seem all glossy surfaces, all tinsel and glitter, but contributing to that surface are a complex tension of narrative and number, a problematic or "impossible" relation to the realistic codes that dominate most mainstream fare, a formal and thematic investment in musicality, an enduring relation to popular music and other forms of musical entertainment, and a celebration of stars' talents. Some viewers may hold up the integrated style as the gold standard, while others may appreciate the looser pleasures of the aggregated style, which follows from a vaudeville aesthetic. Not all musicals feature characters bursting into song or dancing in the street, to be sure, but all musicals showcase musical performances. And even while numbers serve the narrative by advancing it in some fashion, the narrative in every musical works in varying ways to "hang together" the numbers.

Traditional musicals exist on a continuum with dramas having some musical sequences at one extreme and biopics and documentaries about musical performers and composers at the other. This continuum respects the formal rigidity of the genre's conventions—most musicals have an underlying sameness that identifies them as "musicals"—while illuminating their flexibility. This guidebook will glance now and then at the end points of that continuum while focusing on musicals clustered in the middle. Moreover, throughout I emphasize musicals of the studio era, along with their stars and directors, because they are less well-known to most contemporary viewers and, in my view, are well worth learning about and rediscovering today. Older musicals most readily illustrate how the genre works in its traditional forms. They establish conventions that some contemporary musicals play against or efface even while displaying signs of their lineage in the genre, while those older examples also make evident the resonances of their music-ality that carry over into other genres, like the action film.

2

A BRIEF ACCOUNT OF THE LONG HISTORY OF THE HOLLYWOOD MUSICAL

Common lore has it that the American film industry fully converted to sound immediately following the smash success of Warner Bros.' *The Jazz Singer* (1927) starring Al Jolson. Or at least that is how *Singin' in the Rain* (1952) memorably recounts it. For in that musical almost as soon as *The Jazz Singer* opens in October 1927, the fictional studio Monumental Pictures shuts down all of its silent films then in production, installs sound equipment, and begins shooting talkies, although not without some hilarious problems.

Actually, the process by which Hollywood converted to talking pictures was somewhat slower and more cautious. First of all, *The Jazz Singer* was not a full-fledged talkie but a mostly silent picture with several songs added and a few lines recorded of (supposedly) ad-libbed dialogue. Second, the huge returns of *The Singin' Fool* (1928), Warners' follow-up with Jolson, is what convinced Hollywood that sound was not a flash in the pan. It was not until 1929 that the studios began to release a full season of talkies to theaters, at which point there was no going back and, given box-office receipts, no reason to do so. Third, three different sound processes were in play in the late 1920s: Warners'

Vitaphone recorded sound on discs to be played in sync with the film in theatres (the method shown in *Singin' in the Rain*), while Western Electric (the manufacturing sector of American Telegraph and Telephone) and Radio Corporation of America (co-owned by General Electric and Westinghouse) each had an optical sound-on-film process. In that method, recorded sound was converted to a line of light on the celluloid for the projector to translate and play back through a speaker. Vitaphone yielded a more dynamic recording but, as *Singin' in the Rain* hilariously recalls, it was also subject to voices going out of sync with the picture, whether due to projectionist error or a scratch on the disc. Soon, although the Vitaphone name lingered on Warners' films for a while as a brand, sound-on-film became the industry standard.

The introduction of sound helped to consolidate what we call the Hollywood studio system. Paramount and MGM-Loew's had already controlled production, distribution, and exhibition of their films by 1927. With profits from their early talkies, Fox, Warner Bros., and RKO-Radio merged with smaller companies, bought regional theater chains, and expanded production facilities to achieve that same degree of control by the early 1930s. The drive to expand would then cause major economic troubles for most studios as the Great Depression continued throughout the decade. For instance, Twentieth Century Pictures merged with the financially struggling Fox Films in 1935 to form Twentieth Century-Fox. In any event, for most of the studio era the major companies had their own flagship theaters downtown in some cities throughout the United States, but each studio dominated a sector of the country through ownership of numerous neighborhood as well as multiple downtown houses. There were exceptions to this configuration, but generally speaking Fox had the West Coast and Rocky Mountain territories, Paramount the Midwest, South, and Southwest, Warners had Pennsylvania and the mid-Atlantic, and RKO and MGM-Loew's shared the East Coast states and Ohio. These five vertically integrated majors were friendly competitors, along with the three "minor" companies (Columbia, Universal, and United Artists), minor because they produced and distributed films but lacked their own exhibition chains. Until the federal government successfully broke up this oligopoly with the Paramount consent decree in 1948 mandating the studios' financial separation from exhibition, this system whereby all aspects of filmmaking were dominated by those five majors and three minor companies defined the manufacturing of motion pictures in the United States.

More to our purposes, as *Singin' in the Rain* also tells it, with the introduction of sound came the birth of the film musical, and this was closer to the truth. Live music had always been an important element in the viewing of silent films, whether provided by a full orchestra or band in downtown movie palaces or by the versatility of a pipe organ in smaller venues. Although some stage operettas such as *The Merry Widow* (1925) were filmed as silent pictures, once sound became the norm for movies the film musical was made possible and, as *Singin' in the Rain* shows, bound to happen.

With a few exceptions, the first wave of musicals were cumbersome affairs as studios had to learn how to use sound effectively when filming numbers, how to position actors in relation to the microphone, how to conceal the live orchestra, and how to choreograph dancing for the camera now that it was confined to the "icebox." Each studio produced lavish revues, such as MGM's *Hollywood Revue* (1929), Warners' *Show of Shows* (1929) and *On With the Show* (1929), and Universal's *King of Jazz* (1930). Not all early musicals were revues, though. After MGM's *The Broadway Melody* (1929)—the first "all talking, all singing, all dancing" picture as its poster declared—won the Academy Award for Best Picture, musicals with fictional narratives were initially very popular, if only for their novelty's sake. And some, like the ones that Ziegfeld Follies star Eddie Cantor did for independent producer Samuel Goldwyn and United Artists, stood out for its cast, with many players in addition to Cantor imported from the stage, and for Busby Berkeley's early efforts at filming dance numbers. Beginning with the successful film version of his Broadway hit, *Whoopee!* (1930), Goldwyn brought out a new musical with Cantor almost yearly until 1936. Moreover, with *The Love Parade* (1929) director

Ernst Lubitsch at Paramount is credited with first understanding how to put together numbers and narrative in musicals that were not set backstage, showing the way as well for what became the integrated film musical. But overall, audiences soon tired of the genre for its sameness and clumsiness. Some musicals, in fact, had their numbers removed prior to release due to audience disinterest in the genre; and a formally innovative musical such as Rouben Mamoulian's Love Me Tonight (1932), which like The Love Parade showed everything the genre could and would go on to do, was a box-office disappointment for Paramount.

In 1933 Warner Bros. revived the musical's popularity with a series of backstagers distinguished by Berkeley's eye-popping numbers and featuring many of the same players such as Ruby Keeler, Dick Powell, and Joan Blondell, along with character actors Guy Kibbee and Hugh Hubert: 42nd Street (1933), Gold Diggers of 1933 (1933), Footlight Parade (1933), Dames (1934), and Gold Diggers of 1935 (1935). This cycle continued at Warners for the rest of the decade, and Berkeley's over-the-top style was imitated elsewhere though rarely equaled. At around the same time, RKO signed Broadway star Fred Astaire, who began his series of musicals opposite Ginger Rogers. Introduced as a dancing couple in Flying Down to Rio (1933), the pair top-billed some of the decade's most popular films, such as The Gay Divorcee (1934), Top Hat (1935), and Swing Time (1936). Astaire had contractual control over the filming and editing of his dance numbers, and he set the example for filming performers dancing in full body shots with very few edits that would be the norm for many decades afterward.

Paramount, which had begun the decade with Maurice Chevalier and Jeanette MacDonald in popular operetta-styled musicals until the failure of their Love Me Tonight, starred Mae West and the Marx Brothers in a series of musicals, some based on their hit plays, and brought Bing Crosby and Bob Hope to the screen in the studio's cycle of Big Broadcast musicals (1932, 1935, 1936, 1938) that exploited radio's popularity. Fox did skating musicals with Olympics athlete Sonja Henie, wildly successful children's musicals with Shirley Temple, and slowly developed Alice Faye as a major singing star of films. Universal had the teenage Deanna Durbin, whose musicals (along with horror films) kept the studio alive financially.

Not to be undone, MGM produced *Dancing Lady* (1933) with Joan Crawford and Clark Gable to rival *42nd Street* but found greater success with dancer Eleanor Powell, who toplined a series through the early 1940s beginning with *Broadway Melody of 1936* (1935), *Born to Dance* (1936), and *Broadway Melody of 1938* (1937), the last featuring a young Judy Garland. At the same time, with *Naughty Marietta* (1935) and *Rose-Marie* (1936), MGM began an equally successful string of operettas starring Jeanette MacDonald, who moved to the studio from Paramount, and Nelson Eddy. By 1939, when it released *The Wizard of Oz* and *Babes in Arms*, both starring the teenage Garland, this studio was quickly becoming the one most identified with the Hollywood film musical, an identity that persisted for the next two decades.

Figure 2.1 Eleanor Powell in *Broadway Melody of 1936* (1935, MGM)

As the musical developed during the 1930s the genre became a bankable star vehicle, with scripts, songs, and dancing crafted to suit the expertise of a particular star or star couple who typically were under long term contracts at their particular studio. In the 1940s Technicolor became a selling point, too, emphasizing the genre's appeal to lavish production values and escapism. The use of color for Oz as a vivid contrast to sepia-tinted black-and-white Kansas in *The Wizard of Oz* anticipated the value color would have for 1940s musicals in distinguishing the genre from standard movie fare like comedies, melodramas, horror, war films, mysteries, and thrillers. Along with musicals, until the early 1950s color was by and large reserved for historical epics, some Westerns, and fantasy.

From 1929 with the Oscar-winning *The Broadway Melody* through 1958 with the Oscar-winning *Gigi*, the Hollywood movie studios turned out dozens of original musicals each year. Studios like Metro-Goldwyn-Mayer and Twentieth Century-Fox each had talented stars and specialty acts under contract, along with directors, composers, writers, choreographers, arrangers, set and costume designers, sound engineers, even their own house orchestras. Because many of these artists frequently worked together on film after film, they formed a kind of studio repertory company, helping to brand an MGM musical or a Fox musical with a distinctive house style. Furthermore, many of that era's musicals were crucial in mainstreaming popular music during the 1930s and 1940s, in particular, jazz ("jazz" in the sense of being fast and syncopated or "hot" music, often combined with the blues and conflated with swing) as performed onscreen by one of the Big Bands such as Benny Goodman's, Artie Shaw's, and Jimmy or Tommy Dorsey's. During this era, Hollywood musicals exemplified America's popular entertainment.

These three decades—the 1930s, 1940s, and 1950s—were the genre's highpoint in terms of original musicals; as expensive yet reliable product, musicals often made the difference between profit and loss. During this period MGM produced the most lavish, star-studded musicals on an annual basis, averaging something like eight new ones every year until the late 1950s. Judy Garland became its biggest singing star, first opposite Mickey Rooney in teen backstage musicals following the success of their *Babes in Arms*, then as an above-the-title star in her own right with *Meet Me in St. Louis* (1944) and *The Harvey Girls* (1946). At MGM Eleanor Powell, Ann Sothern, and Esther Williams also had star vehicles designed for them. Williams in particular was neither a great singer or dancer, but she could swim and her colorful "aqua-musicals," which popularized synchronized swimming as an art form, were among the studio's most successful. Additionally, Metro had Ann Miller, Betty Garrett, and Virginia O'Brien, all talents in their own right, for secondary roles.

Along with Rooney and George Murphy, who became stars during the 1930s, and Astaire who worked here on a freelance basis at this studio in the 1940s and 1950s, MGM signed Gene Kelly, Frank Sinatra, and Red Skelton, designing musicals around the special skills of each (respectively: dancing, singing, comedy). After Garland left the studio in 1950 and following the successes of *Anchors Aweigh* (1945), *On the Town* (1949), *An American in Paris* (1951), and *Singin' in the Rain*, Kelly, who choreographed his numbers and codirected some of his musicals with Stanley Donen, became the star most identified with MGM's output. Metro continued to groom new musical talent in the late 1940s and early 1950s, too: Kathryn Grayson, Howard Keel, Jane Powell, Cyd Charisse, Debbie Reynolds, Leslie Caron, Marge and Gower Champion, Bobby Van, and Bob Fosse starred or were featured in MGM's musicals.

During this period other studios, while not as deep as MGM in their stables of contract performers, similarly crafted musicals to suit the talents of their own stars. Fox was perhaps MGM's most direct competitor with popular Technicolor musicals starring Alice Faye or Betty Grable, often costarring them with Carmen Miranda, and pairing them with John Payne, Don Ameche, or Dan Dailey. Of those men, Dailey was the most versatile when it came to musicals since he could sing and dance. Additionally, June Haver, Vivian Blaine, Mitzi Gaynor, and Marilyn Monroe were groomed as eventual replacements for Grable, whose unsurpassed popularity in the 1940s kept almost all her musicals in the black. Monroe became a big star after *Gentlemen Prefer Blondes* (1953), equaling Grable's status at the box-office. In addition to Crosby and Hope, who topped box-office polls almost every year during the 1940s and who costarred in the popular series of "Road" musical comedies with Dorothy Lamour, Paramount hired band singer Betty Hutton, who crossed over to starring roles. In the 1950s the studio produced musical comedies with Dean Martin and Jerry Lewis until the team broke up in 1956. Aside from several biopics about performers or composers and musical comedies with Jack Carson and Dennis Morgan in an effort to compete with Paramount's Hope and Crosby, Warner Bros did not produce as many musicals as they had done in the 1930s until they signed band singer Doris Day for *Romance on the High* Seas (1948), after which she toplined numerous ones during her seven years at this studio, costarring with Gordon McCrae in several. Warners also had dancer Gene Nelson under contract.

As for the smaller companies, Columbia had Rita Hayworth, who initially costarred in two musicals with Astaire and one with Kelly and afterwards was the main attraction in her films. This studio also produced a series of low-budget musicals with Ann Miller before she moved to MGM in 1948. Along with Durbin, Universal had a young Donald O'Connor under contract, featuring him in its series of low-budget musicals until O'Connor went freelance in the 1950s and became a reliable costar with Kelly in *Singin' in the Rain* and Crosby in *Anything Goes* (1956). Goldwyn, who now distributed his films through RKO, signed Danny Kaye, who had made a name for himself on Broadway and in nightclubs, building successful musicals from *Up in Arms* (1944) to *Hans Christian Andersen* (1952) around his eccentric but multifaceted talents as a performer. In addition, Kaye toplined musicals for Warners, Fox, Paramount, and MGM.

Another element that went into musicals from the 1930s, 1940s, and 1950s were the talents of notable songwriters from Broadway who wrote first-rate original scores that have since yielded many familiar standards in the pop music song catalogue. Irving Berlin wrote new songs for Astaire in *Top Hat, Follow the Fleet* (1935), *Carefree* (1938), *Holiday Inn* (1942), *Blue Skies* (1946), and *Easter Parade* (1948). George and Ira Gershwin wrote scores for Astaire's *Shall We Dance* (1937) and *Damsel in Distress* (1937), and Jerome Kern and Dorothy Fields wrote the numbers for his *Swing Time*. Cole Porter composed original songs for numerous MGM films: *Born to Dance* and *Rosalie* (1937) with Powell, *Broadway Melody of 1940* (1940) with Astaire and Powell, *The Pirate* (1948) with Garland and Kelly, *High Society* (1956) with Crosby and Sinatra, and *Les Girls* (1957) with Kelly and Mitzi Gaynor. Fresh from their Broadway bonanza called *My Fair Lady*, Alan Jay Lerner and Frederick Loewe wrote *Gigi* for MGM. For Rita Hayworth's musicals, Columbia hired Porter for *You'll Never Get Rich* (1941), Kern and Johnny Mercer for *You Were Never Lovelier* (1942), Kern and Ira Gershwin for *Cover Girl* (1942), and Jule Styne and Sammy Kahn for *Tonight and Every Night* (1945). At Paramount, Jimmy Van Heusen and Johnny Burke wrote scores for the Hope and Crosby's "Road" movies, and the studio used Frank Loesser, Jule Styne, Harold Arlen, Sammy Cahn, Hoagy Carmichael, Paul Francis Webster, Jay Livingston, and Ray Evans on various Betty Hutton vehicles. Competing with MGM's *Meet Me in St. Louis*, Twentieth Century-Fox produced two folk musicals, *State Fair* (1945) with a score by Richard Rodgers and Oscar Hammerstein II and *Centennial Summer* (1946) with one by Kern and multiple lyricists. Harry Warren and Mack David wrote for many of the studio's musicals with Grable or Faye, such as *Down Argentine Way* (1940), *Week-End in Havana* (1941), and *Springtime in the Rockies* (1942).

Many songwriters migrated from one studio to another, too. For instance, Johnny Mercer and Harold Arlen wrote the score for Paramount's *Here Come the Waves* (1944), Mercer and Harry Warren wrote scores for MGM's *The Harvey Girls* and *The Belle of New York* (1951), Mercer and Gene de Paul wrote the score for that studio's *Seven Brides for Seven Brothers* (1954), and Mercer wrote both music and lyrics for Fox's *Daddy Long Legs* (1955).

Even when a studio purchased rights to a stage success, rarely was the entire score used; rather, while retaining one or two of the most familiar songs from the stage version, the studio would typically commission a new score from its in-house songsmiths. MGM's *DuBarry Was a Lady* (1943) used only three songs from Cole Porter's Broadway score, replacing the rest with new songs by Burton Lane, Ralph Freed, E. Y. Harburg, and Roger Edens. In addition to using its own stars then under contract (Lucille Ball, Red Skelton, Gene Kelly, Virginia O'Brien), the studio added singing groups, The Pied Pipers and The Three Oxford Boys, and Tommy Dorsey's orchestra to perform some of the numbers. Starting in the 1950s, however, more faithful adaptation of Broadway musicals were produced, reflecting how the integration aesthetic had become a norm onstage for shows with a strong book and mostly integrated numbers. MGM's *Annie Get Your Gun* (1950) and *Kiss Me Kate* (1953) kept most of their Broadway scores intact, as did Warners' *The Pajama Game* (1956) and *Damn Yankees* (1957), Paramount's *Lil Abner* (1959), and the adaptations of Rodgers and Hammerstein's hits produced or distributed by Fox, *Oklahoma* (1955), *Carousel* (1956), *The King and* I (1956), and *South Pacific* (1957).

One advantage for the studios of owning original scores, though, was their control of the publishing and, eventually, recording rights, a boon when studios like MGM created their own record label in 1946. Moreover, studios recycled their songs in subsequent musicals and as background music in other genres as well. Paramount used Rodgers and Hart's "Isn't It Romantic?," initially in *Love Me Tonight*, in many subsequent films to connote "romance" on the soundtrack. Additionally, studios created musicals from catalogues of songs they owned outright or licensed. Catalogue musicals were a forerunner of Broadway's jukebox musicals; both build a narrative out of older, well-known songs from other sources. At MGM *Till the Clouds Roll By* (1946) featured the Kern song catalogue, *Words and Music* (1948) that of Rodgers and Hart, *An American in Paris* that of the Gershwins, and *Singin' in the Rain* that of Arthur Freed and Nacio Herb Brown, who had written many new songs for the studio's early musicals. At Warners biopics like *Rhapsody in Blue* (1945), a fictionalized account of George Gershwin's life, and *Night and Day* (1946), an equally fictionalized account of Cole Porter's, reused their subject's song catalogues. Fox did two big budget Irving Berlin catalogue musicals, *Alexander's Ragtime Band* (1938) and *There's No Business Like Show Business* (1954). Some catalogue musicals interpolated new songs into the assortment of old ones. MGM's *Easter Parade* and Paramount's *Blue Skies* (1946) and *White Christmas* (1954) mix new and old Berlin tunes.

Along with its large cohort of onscreen talent, MGM had the most directors specializing in musicals during the studio era, and their names have also become synonymous with the genre: Vincente Minnelli (*Meet Me in St. Louis, An American in Paris*), Charles Walters (*Easter Parade, High Society*), Stanley Donen (*Royal Wedding* [1951]), *Seven Brides for Seven Brothers*), and George Sidney (*The Harvey Girls, Show Boat* [1951]). Following his tenure at Warners, Busby Berkeley went to MGM, where he directed Rooney and Garland and also Esther Williams, but he also made a single picture for Fox, *The Gang's All Here* (1943). As the studio system saw its ending during the late 1950s Donen went on to direct *Funny Face* (1957) at Paramount and to codirect two musicals at Warners with legendary Broadway director George Abbot, *The Pajama Game* and *Damn Yankees*. Sidney made several musicals for Columbia, notably *Pal Joey* (1957) and *Bye Bye Birdie* (1963).

Metro was not alone in having in-house directors skilled in the musical genre, and just like that studio's directors, their work was not limited to this one genre. With the coming of sound as noted earlier, silent film director Ernst Lubitsch made several innovative musicals at Paramount starring Chevalier and/or MacDonald (*The Love Parade* [1929], *Monte Carlo* [1930], *The Smiling Lieutenant* [1931], *One Hour with You* [1932]), before moving to MGM where he made *The Merry Widow* (1934) with those two stars. Distinguished Broadway director Rouben Mamoulian made a few musicals at Paramount (*Applause* [1929], *Love Me Tonight, High Wide and Handsome* [1937]), returning to Hollywood years later after several major stage successes (e.g., *Oklahoma!, Carousel*) when he made *Summer Holiday* (1948) and *Silk Stockings* (1957) at MGM. Mark Sandrich made five musicals with Astaire and Rodgers at RKO (*The Gay Divorcee, Top Hat, Follow the Fleet* [1936], *Swing Time* [1936], *Carefree* [1937]), and moved to Paramount in the early 1940s where he directed *Holiday Inn* and *Here Comes the Waves* (1944). Sandrich passed away while working on *Blue Skies*.

Berkeley created the distinctive style of numbers in Warner Bros musicals in the 1930s. After he left, Warners used David Butler as its go-to person for many musicals but also had Michael Curtiz behind the camera for a handful of musical biopics and four Doris Day musicals. Curtiz went on to direct *White Christmas* for Paramount. At Fox, Walter Lang directed over a dozen musicals, from vehicles for Faye and Grable in the 1940s to adaptations of Broadway hits in the 1950s, *Call Me Madam* (1953) and *The King and* I. Additionally, choreographers like Jack Cole at Fox primarily but also at Columbia and MGM, Robert Alton at MGM, Danny Dare at Paramount, and freelancers Hermes Pan and Michael Kidd staged dance numbers. Gower Champion and Bob Fosse, later to become major Broadway director-choreographers, also staged their own dances. After leaving MGM and before returning to films as a director with *Cabaret* (1972), Fosse choreographed *My Sister Eileen* (1955) for Columbia and, recreating his work on stage, *The Pajama Game* and *Damn Yankees* for Warners.

The studio system was geared toward giving producers a great deal of authority from casting to script supervision to final print approval, and musicals were no exception. The most famous producer of the genre was Arthur Freed at MGM, whose production unit, a team of collaborative above- and below-the-line craftspeople and artisans, made *Meet Me in St. Louis, The Harvey Girls, Easter Parade, On the Town, An American in Paris, Singin' in the Rain,* and *The Band Wagon* (1953). Freed's music arranger, songwriter, and associate producer Roger Edens nurtured young talent like Judy Garland, who matured into a triple-threat talent in Freed musicals during the 1940s. Freed himself brought to Hollywood artists from the Broadway stage, such as Minnelli and the team of Betty Comden and Adolph Green, who wrote lyrics and screenplays. The Freed unit was so successful and such a tight group of people working together that at MGM they were called, after the blockbuster Christmas-time opening of *On the Town* at Radio City Music Hall, "the Royal Family."

Befitting a studio so committed to the genre, MGM also had other producers, Joe Pasternak (who moved to the studio in 1942 from Universal, where he had overseen Deanna Durbin's musicals) and Jack Cummings, shepherding musicals from the planning stage to their release. At Fox, William Perlberg and William Le Baron each produced many of this studio's 1940s musicals. Sol C. Siegel began at Paramount, moved to Fox in the late 1940s, and left there in the mid-1950s for MGM. Buddy DeSylva, another songwriter, produced musicals along with other genres at Paramount. William Jacobs supervised a number of musicals at Warners.

While some women worked behind the scenes—just at MGM, for example, Betty Comden and Frances Goodrich wrote scripts with their male collaborators, Kay Thompson did vocal arrangements and also helped to shape Garland's and Lena Horne's sophisticated singing style, Adrienne Fazan edited numerous musicals, Margaret Booth was the studio's supervising editor, and Irene Sharaff did costumes and some scenic designs for several—the classic Hollywood musical was pretty much made by men. They directed films, wrote scores, staged dances, ran cameras, supervised lighting, designed sets, orchestrated music and recorded and mixed sound.

However, a reliance on a mixed gay and straight workforce behind the scenes and the import of so many female stars in front of the camera accounts for how and why this era's musicals differ from other genres in their treatment of men and women. Generally speaking, and with the exception of the melodramatic "woman's films" of the 1930s and 1940s and some comedies, male protagonists drove the plots of standard studio-era movies with female characters placed in passive roles as objects of male desire or threats to its fulfillment. To be sure, the narratives of musicals frequently close by subordinating the female lead to her male counterpart, reflecting how the genre still reiterated the era's dominant ideology about active masculinities, passive femininities, and a focus on the romantic heterosexual couple. Furthermore, show musicals typically featured women in semirevealing costumes that highlighted breasts, crotches, and legs. Even major stars like Grable and Hayworth were promoted for their looks more than their talent. And today the two people in front of the camera who are most remembered for their innovations in pushing the musical to its artistic heights are Astaire and Kelly, whose influence is undeniable.

But that the musical genre primarily served as a star vehicle for women tells another story about its appeal. As Adrienne McLean explains, "When a woman begins to sing, as well as dance, she can become a point of identification and community, in addition to, or possibly instead of, a figure or object representing only sexual difference" (McLean 2005: 126). While many studio-era musicals were designed for Crosby, Kaye, Astaire, and Kelly (and before them, for Jolson and Cantor), many more were crafted for female stars playing characters who drive the narrative alone or in concert with a male costar in what McLean calls "women's musicals" (112): Eleanor Powell, Jeanette MacDonald, Judy Garland, Esther Williams, Betty Grable, Alice Faye, Rita Hayworth, Betty Hutton, and Doris Day. Plots of their musicals pivot around the actions and desires of the female lead so that, even if she gets her comeuppance in the final moments, she is still the central figure carrying the musical or when, as in some of Grable's musicals, say, like *Coney Island* (1943), her character is subordinated in the narrative to the schemes of a male costar, she carries the numbers, the source of the films' energy and imagination.

Whether singing or dancing, a female star has ample opportunities to express her subjectivity as a character musically—her desires, her fears, her goals and ambitions, her spiritedness—and to do so directly to the audience, even when her performance is framed as an onscreen show number. Additionally, talented female performers like Ann Miller and Virginia O'Brien at MGM, or Charlotte Greenwood and Carmen Miranda at Fox, were often featured alongside the major stars with solo numbers of their own, further emphasizing a focus on the women as independent, active musical subjects. Women, in sum, energized musicals, which still accounts for the genre's strong following among women and girls as well as its historical appeal to gay male fans, who saw in those female stars an alternative to what they experienced as an oppressive standard of heteromasculinity that movies (not to say their culture) otherwise reiterated.

The popularity of Carmen Miranda during the 1940s raises another way to think about what made studio-era musicals different and at times provocative. During an era when ethnic and racial minorities were marginalized if not altogether absent on screen, musicals opened spaces for nonwhite, non-Christian performers. The contributions of great Jewish songwriters for musicals—Berlin, Gershwin, Rodgers, Hart, Hammerstein, and so on—goes without saying. While movie stars of different ethnic backgrounds typically had their names changed and bios adjusted to appear more Anglicized, Jolson, Cantor, Fanny Brice, and Sophie Tucker still made for a noticeably visible Jewish presence in 1930s musicals, much as did Danny Kaye (born Kaminsky) in the 1940s and 1950s, and Barbra Streisand in the late 1960s. Without disguising their ethnic backgrounds, Latin actors such as Delores Del Rio, Caesar Romero, Ricardo Montalban, and Fernando Lamas as well as Miranda were cast in major roles opposite white performers and showcased in numbers that, even when the music, costumes, settings, and their diction were mediated by stereotypes of Latinness, still invested their Latin characters with a sense of energy and purpose. Xavier Cugat at MGM epitomized the new popularity of Latin music in the 1940s as the Big Band sound began to wane.

The presence of African American performers in musicals, on the other hand, was more restricted. A black film community existed outside of Hollywood, making what were called at the time "race films" for exhibition at segregated black theatres, and these included musicals such as Hi De Ho (1947), Sepia Cinderella (1947), and Boarding House Blues (1948). As for black stars in mainstream musicals, Bill Robinson danced with Shirley Temple in several 1930s films at Fox and starred in that studio's Stormy Weather (1943), a musical showcasing numerous African American performers. Paul Robeson was a memorable Bill in Show Boat (1936), but his radical politics derailed his career in Hollywood.

Black artists still appeared frequently in numbers even though not playing characters. Sean Griffin has pointed out that a vaudeville aesthetic enabled a number of black performers to appear regularly as specialty acts in Fox musicals of the 1940s, thereby causing gaps in the films' otherwise white surface "through which various hegemonic norms [could] be momentarily critiqued and upended" (Griffin 2002, 31). With the Nicholas Brothers under contract, Fox musicals stand out in this regard, but black entertainers—such as Cab Calloway, Hazel Scott, Avon Long, the Berry Brothers, and Louis Armstrong to name a few—did their specialties there and in other studios' musicals too. MGM made a star of Lena Horne in the 1940s but had difficulty fitting her into narratives as a character, treating her instead as a specialty act in one or two numbers that bracketed her from her white costars. Horne played characters in two all-black musicals, her studio's *Cabin in the Sky* (1943) and opposite Robinson in Fox's *Stormy Weather*; she also played Julie in an abbreviated version of the first act of *Show Boat* in MGM's *Till the Clouds Roll By* (a part played by Ava Gardner when MGM remade the musical in 1951). In the 1950s Dorothy Dandridge had somewhat better luck than Horne in getting plum narrative roles at Fox; though few were musicals, she did receive an Oscar nomination as the lead of *Carmen Jones* (1954).

STORMY WEATHER (1943)

Although it is a rare all–African American film produced by a major Hollywood studio, and the only studio-produced black musical that does not have a folk setting, on the face of it *Stormy Weather* is a typical Twentieth Century-Fox backstager. Framed in the present day when tap dancer Bill Williamson (Bill Robinson) receives in the mail a special edition of *Theatre World* celebrating his long career, the narrative of *Stormy Weather* traces Bill's life, beginning with his return from Europe at the end of World War II, taking him through to his stage and then Hollywood success, and finally ending again in the present day at a World War II fundraising revue. During those twenty-five years Bill meets, loses, meets again, loses again, and finally reunites with singer

Selina Rogers (Lena Horne), the two stars never aging a day (despite the considerable difference in the stars' real ages), their agelessness also a convention of Fox's backstage musicals.

Along the way Bill encounters real-life black entertainers who play themselves or barely fictionalized versions of themselves and who perform numbers that display their special talents: Cab Calloway, Katherine Dunham and her dance company, Fats Waller, Ada Brown, Dooley Wilson, Mae Johnson, Emmett 'Babe' Wallace, and the Nicholas Brothers. With some sixteen numbers, several orchestral versions of other songs, and a few reprises packed into its 78 minutes, *Stormy Weather* can be considered a filmed revue, too, its fictional biopic serving to hang the numbers together and to provide bridges to take viewers from one period in Bill's musical life to the next. Although the film had a white director in Andrew Stone and many songs were written by white composers influenced by jazz or the blues, Irving Mills, who was white but had managed and recorded Calloway and Duke Ellington, produced *Stormy Weather*, and in addition to black entertainers like Waller and Calloway who performed their own distinctive style in their specialty spots, Dunham choreographed her dance troupe in the ballet section of the title song, Clarence Robinson staged several other dance numbers, and the Nicholas Brothers no doubt were responsible for their incredible moves, although in most instances just as probably white people dressed the sets and lit and filmed them (Vogel 2008: 104).

Given the period's segregationist practices it also ought not be surprising that the diegesis of *Stormy Weather* is an insular, some might say a fantasy, world where no white people exist, not even as spectators in the nightclub sequences. Furthermore, characterizations are mediated by the era's racist stereotypes of black people. In the first flashback section at the Public Hall celebrating the 15th Regiment's return home from France in 1918, dancers do the cakewalk, a strolling dance that had become mainstreamed and whitened by 1943 but was initially performed by blacks on Southern plantations starting in the late 1860s. While there is no blackface in the musical numbers, costumes show blackface iconography; female dancers in the first section wear hats that resemble big daisies, the backs of which are caricatures of big smiling black faces, so when, in this number's opening, they stand on the tiers of a giant wedding cake with their backs to the audience they look like they are sporting black-face as the men dance around the cake, straw hats held high. At another point, the male dancers bend down in front of the females to mime shining their shoes. Dooley Wilson's shiftless, lying, bragging character Gabe, Bill's best friend, is a repeated source of "humor" in this first flashback section and a later one. And in the second flashback, though worn out from loading bales of cotton on a riverboat traveling the Mississippi to Memphis and lying down to sleep, Bill's feet almost frenetically respond to the live music playing nearby by "those minstrel boys that got on in New Orleans" and, with a wide grin, he cannot resist rising to go dance with them. Later, as part of Bill's own stage revue at some time in the 1930s, Flournoy Miller and Johnnie Lee, African American comedians, do a blackface comedy routine.

Nonetheless, *Stormy Weather* is worth one's close attention. Shane Vogel argues that the overlapping of the stars' real and character first names brings to the film the history of Cotton Club performances, epitomized for him by the complexity of Ethel Waters's modernist rendition of "Stormy Weather" there, which Horne's version and Denham's ballet evoke as a "palimpsest," just as, given all the luminaries featured as specialty acts, "the film provided a vehicle through which the personalities of Jazz Age Harlem performed their own mythology" (Vogel 2008: 104). In Vogel's account, *Stormy Weather* looks backward in its musical numbers yet many numbers offer possibilities of critiquing Hollywood's conditions for representing blackness (105). As important, as performed and in the mis-en-scene, Stormy Weather offers a history of black entertainment from minstrelsy to modernism, from primitivism to sophistication; and given its rich repertoire of musical styles, this is also to say that, in its numerous show numbers, the musical records how American popular music during the first four decades of the past century had its sources in black culture. The testament to Bill on the cover of Theatre World—"celebrating the magnificent contribution of the colored race to the entertainment of the world during the past twenty-five years"—could equally apply to the music as well as the man.

If we follow the narrative trajectory, we see how it travels from the Public Hall, where a modified Black Bottom dance by Bill, Selina, and the ensemble precedes the blackface-inspired cakewalk dancing, to the river boat, where Robinson does an impromptu dance to "Dah, Dat, Dah" with The Tramp Band, and from there to a Beale Street blues dive bar run by Ada Brown, where she and Fats Waller perform one bluesy number, "That Ain't Right," and Waller performs his signature tune, "Ain't Misbehavin," with his syncopated piano playing, his band's jazzy impromptu breaks, and a customer comically dancing the shuffle. At Ada's, Bill meets Selina again and she convinces Chick Bailey (Wallace) to include Bill as a dancer in his new show. The show's two big numbers finds its visual motifs in the African primitivism that characterized 1920s modernism and was a central design element of many Cotton Club shows. Selina sings and writhes to "Diga Diga Do" in native costume, supported by showgirls dressed as cats, while Bill, dressed as a jungle tribesman and seated in a tree, beats a bongo; and in "African Dance" sung by Bailey, Bill steals the show by tap dancing bare-chested across the jungle set from one giant drum to another.

Figure 2.2 Bill Robinson dancing to "Dah, Dat, Dah" with The Tramp Band in *Stormy Weather* (1943, Twentieth Century-Fox)

Figure 2.3 Lena Horne singing "Diga Diga Do" in *Stormy Weather* (1943, Twentieth Century-Fox)

In the next sequence Bill has pulled together a revue of his own, though not without money troubles. Gabe shows up and pretends he is a rich backer. Backstage, Mae Johnson performs a bluesey "I Lost My Sugar in Salt Lake City," followed by an unidentified dancer's fast, athletic solo to "Nobody's Sweetheart." The next sequence features Bill and Selina in full Astaire and Rogers mode as, he in tails and she in a long shimmering white gown, sing and dance to "I Can't Give You Anything but Love." Thereafter they separate because he wants to settle down in marriage but, all along expressing her ambition which exceeds his, she does not want to give up her career to become a wife and mother. Back in the present day, Cab Calloway invites Bill to his revue, in which he performs "Geechy Joe" in his sexually provocative manner; Selina sings a plaintive "Stormy Weather" (setting up her reunion with Bill when she spies him in the audience), which bookends Dunham's ballet version; Selina and Bill reconnect in a reprise with Calloway of "There's No Two Ways about Love"; Bill sings "My, My Ain't that Somethin'"; and finally, after Calloway introduces "Jumpin' Jive," the dancing Nicholas Brothers defy gravity with their jumping and jiving to that music. In the finale, Bill and Selina confirm their reunion with "My, My Ain't that Somethin'."

Figure 2.4 Bill Robinson and Lena Horne perform "I Can't Give You Anything But Love" in *Stormy Weather* (1943, Twentieth Century-Fox)

Figure 2.5 Cab Calloway and the Nicholas Brothers do the "Jumpin' Jive" in *Stormy Weather* (1943, Twentieth Century-Fox)

As evident in the numbers' changing styles, with Bill and Selina acquiring ever greater sophistication in their costuming and performance venues, the narrative's historical progression is purposeful, though to be sure a few numbers stand out stylistically for breaking with a sense of moving through history. For instance, in that first flashback section before the cakewalk number, Horne's performs her first solo, "There's No Two Ways about Love" in the same restrained vocal style that typifies her inserted numbers in MGM musicals of the 1940s, though vocally and physically she loosens up in her singing and dancing in later numbers. "Ain't that Right," a number in the flashback section set in 1919 or 1920 was first recorded in 1942. But by the film's end, with Calloway in his zoot suit and the Nicholas Brothers' dancing, "a subversive cultural politics of style, one dedicated not just to enduring or having fun, but also to demanding and commanding recognition. As *Stormy Weather*'s final number would have it, My my, ain't that something?" (Knight 2002: 158).

Blackness was a vexed, highly conflicted sign in studio-era musicals as evident in how often the genre conventionally cited minstrelsy, an entertainment tradition which became widespread during the nineteenth century and continued into the early twentieth. A minstrel show featured whites in blackface performing stock caricatures of black people. The format had three parts. It began with an Interlocutor serving as MC, the entire cast sitting and singing in a semi-circle on stage, dominated by the comic figures of Mr. Tambo and Mr. Bones (named for their musical instruments, the tambourine and clappers or bone castinets, respectively), each positioned at one end of the semicircle, exchanging jokes and singing humorous songs; a second part, the olio, featured an assortment of musical acts to allow for the scenery to be changed for the third part, a plantation skit or parody of Shakespeare or some other playwright's familiar work. Although blackface performances initially began as a platform for young, working class white street performers to engage in carnivalesque behavior, mocking their bosses and betters (in ways that some scholars say resembles today's hip hop), it became a means of reiterating and drawing humor from unflattering, racist representations of African Americans. Yet all-black minstrel shows also toured the country.

The centrality of minstrelsy to popular culture in the first decades of the twentieth century persisted beyond the format itself. The stock figures provided the characterizations for maids, butlers, bootblacks, and porters as portrayed by black actors in films, for instance. Blackface itself, adhering to those racist stereotypes in makeup, hand gestures, body movement, and diction, became a powerful theatrical trope for white performers, in no small way because it enabled Jewish comics and singers to evade their own marginalized ethnicity on stage (see Rogin 1996). Jolson and Cantor, for example, made blackface a signature of their stage performances and carried it over to their films.

In film musicals, moreover, blackface and minstrelsy were repeatedly used to evoke the unbroken continuity of the nation's popular music going back to the nation's folk music and marking a distinctive tradition that was not European but distinctly American. In many respects this convention indirectly reflects the origins of American popular song in the syncopated sounds of jazz and the blues. Astaire, Crosby, Garland, Rooney, Grable all performed in blackface numbers. When musicals such as *Babes in Arms* and *Babes on Broadway* (1941) recreate minstrel shows for the screen they treat it as shorthand for American entertainment; by performing in blackface, Garland and Rooney absorb the energy of black entertainers while effacing popular music's sources in black culture. The same effect occurs over a decade later in *White Christmas*, which contains probably the last minstrel number in a major Hollywood musical. Without donning blackface yet making use of a stylized yet unmistakable blackface iconography, Crosby and Kaye portray Tambo and Bones in "I'd Rather See a Minstrel Show" while Rosemary Clooney sings the Interlocutor role. As a throwback to minstrel days, the number then segues into "Mandy," written by Irving Berlin in 1919 and previously performed as a blackface number in *This is the Army* (1943).

In many respects when white stars performed blackface they were "covering" music inspired by or directly hailing from black culture, much as white rock-and-roll artists like Elvis Presley did in the 1950s. As the Tin Pan Alley style of original musicals lost its dominance over

Figure 2.6 Bing Crosby, Rosemary Clooney, and Danny Kaye in the minstrel show number from *White Christmas* (1954, Paramount)

popular music in this decade, the movie studios turned to those white recording artists, whose hit records softened the harder rock sound of black musicians and singers, in an effort to recapture the teen market. Paramount signed Presley, eventually sharing him with MGM and Twentieth Century Fox, and Fox also signed Pat Boone, Tommy Sands, and Fabian. These singers starred in musicals such as Presley's *Jailhouse Rock* (1957) and *King Creole* (1958), Boone's *April Love* (1957) and *Mardi Gras* (1958), Sands's *Sing, Boy, Sing* (1958) and *Mardi Gras*, and Fabian's *Hound Dog Man* (1958). However, only Presley had a lasting film career, making musicals through the end of the 1960s. During this period, too, Fox featured white and black recording artists in *The Girl Can't Help It* (1956), a comedy that showcased Little Richard and other singers in several numbers. An independent company brought out *Rock, Rock, Rock* (1956), which gave Chuck Berry a star turn. Columbia released several low-budget musicals, notably *Rock Around the Clock* (1956) and *Don't Knock the Rock* (1956), which featured numerous recording artists as their drawing card. After Chubby Checker popularized the Twist, the studio starred him in *Twist Around the Clock* (1961) and *Don't Knock the Twist* (1962), these titles self-consciously drawing on the studio's earlier rock musicals. In the 1960s, American-International Pictures picked up the slack with its cycle of whiter teen beach musicals, beginning with *Beach Party* (1963) starring singer Frankie Avalon and Annette Funicello, whose career had started in the 1950s on the *Mickey Mouse Club* television show for Disney. In that decade, too, new musical groups like the Monkees, Sonny and Cher, and most successfully the Beatles were given big screen treatments albeit in British-produced musicals.

JAILHOUSE ROCK (1957)

Jailhouse Rock was Elvis Presley's third film, made after *Love Me Tender* (1956) and *Loving You* (1957), and it was known for its iconic title song, which hit the top of the charts, and for enabling Presley to display his potential as an actor. He followed this musical with *King Creole* (1958), which further demonstrated some acting chops, but he was then drafted into the army (the event inspiring the plot of the 1960 stage hit and 1963 film *Bye Bye Birdie*). After his discharge two years later, Presley's manager, "Colonel Tom" Parker, shoehorned him into increasingly formulaic parts that, with few exceptions (such as *GI Blues* (1960) opposite the dancer Juliet Prowse and *Viva Las Vegas* (1964) opposite Ann-Margret), made money and sold records but were unexceptional vehicles that did not stretch Presley's talent.

In *Jailhouse Rock* he portrays Vince Everett, who kills a man with his fists when he tries to stop him from beating a woman in a bar. Convicted of manslaughter, Vince discovers his talent for singing when he appears in a television show broadcast from the prison; released after fourteen months, he begins a singing career and eventually becomes a superstar. *Jailhouse Rock* offers Presley ample opportunity to sing but the narrative is, admittedly, a bit clunky because it establishes the possibility of a serious dramatic conflict early on yet, when it finally arises in the last half hour, this threat is almost immediately dispensed with.

Vince's cell mate, Hunk Houghton (Mickey Shaughnessy), a former country singer, realizes the young man's talent, appeal, and eventual earning potential after the TV appearance when fan mail addressed to Vince floods the prison mail room; arranging to keep him from learning about the mail and exploiting the younger man's naivete, Hunk draws up a contract that will split their future earnings fifty-fifty. Hunk, moreover, describes himself to Vince as "an animal in the jungle," and, he adds, "it's just as bad on the outside. Worse. Remember that." With that warning, after Vince's career takes off with the hit single, "Treat Me Nice," and he partners with Peggy (Judy Tyler) on their own record label, one waits for Hunk's release, expecting him to hold that contract over Vince's head. However, when Hunk finally reappears and reminds Vince of the deal struck in prison, the latter explains that his lawyer says the contract is worthless. Surprisingly, Hunk "the animal" quickly folds, accepting the ten percent Vince offers as a show of gratitude for watching out for him in prison, and he willingly becomes the singer's flunky. Instead, *Jailhouse Rock* shows how success hardens Vince, intensifying his arrogance, egoism, and greed until Hunk literally knocks some sense into him. Starting a fight because of Vince's mistreatment of Peggy, Vince refuses to hit back and in the scuffle Hunk accidentally socks him in the throat, injuring his larynx. In the last few minutes, Vince forgives Hunk, his voice is restored, he embraces Peggy, and all ends happily.

Jailhouse Rock nonetheless stands out as a rare male star-is-born narrative. It incorporates and attempts to crystallize onscreen Presley's early persona as the rock star who fascinated young record-buyers but confused adults. For instance, in the bar scene that results in Vince's manslaughter conviction, both the woman he defends and her abuser comment on his hair; likewise, in prison, his hair gets shorn but it rather quickly grows back into Presley's signature pompadour look. Similarly, the film recognizes Presley's musical origins in country but, as Vince turns to rock, it shows that Hunk's "hillbilly" sound is out of tune with mainstream audiences. And when recording "Don't Leave Me Now," Vince does not find his authentic sound—a fusion of country, R&B, and gospel influences into Presley's innovative rock-and-roll sound—until, as Peggy instructs him, he puts his emotions into the song, to "make it you." What that means for the film, though, is that he drops the guitar he had been playing, which prevented him from moving as he sang—and move he does, just as Presley did (but was prevented from doing on television at that time). The film even anticipates the trajectory of Presley's career: after the television show in which Vince performs "Jailhouse Rock," he moves on to Las Vegas and nightclubs and makes a movie in Hollywood.

Figure 2.7 Elvis Presley performs the title song in *Jailhouse Rock* (1957, MGM)

Moreover, in an appeal to the 1950s teen audience and as Presley's sneering expression seemed to suggest, Vince's outlaw persona as an ex-con connotes not only his being socially rebellious, but it also characterizes him as dangerously sexual. In a memorable scene, Vince aggressively pulls Peggy into a hot kiss. When she gets offended by his "cheap tactics," he kisses her again and replies, "That ain't tactics, honey. It's just the beast in me." Choreographer Alex Romero stages "Jailhouse Rock," the film's only dance number, to showcase Presley's sexually provocative movement as a means of linking his outlaw figure in the film to the 1950s juvenile delinquent—medium shots display Presley with hands in the waist of his pants, his legs swaying, while long shots depict his snapping fingers and thrusting and swiveling body, as the ensemble of dancers follow him up and down the abstract jailhouse set. But *Jailhouse Rock* also characterizes Vince in a manner as suitable to 1950s thinking about domesticated masculinity. Vince is hot tempered and violent, thinking mainly with his fists, and aggressive with and demeaning to women. The film's trajectory, then, is to tame him and, more subtly, tame his music, too, for the last song we hear, as evidence

> of his recovered voice, is his quiet if still full-throated reprise of "Young and Beautiful," his first tentative number in *Jailhouse Rock*, as he stands without much movement behind a piano.

During the 1950s, studios had cut loose longtime stars and other personnel who had been under contract to make musicals, so the genre slowly lost the well-oiled infrastructure that had formerly made it possible to turn out so many original ones on a yearly basis. To be sure, Hollywood continued to make original musicals with big stars like Kelly (*Les Girls*), Astaire (*Daddy Long Legs*), Williams (*Jupiter's Darling* [1955]), and Day (*Lucky Me* [1954]), but as the genre began to lose steam at the box-office and the studios were themselves adjusting to the loss of their profitable theatre chains, Broadway sources became more bankable.

Successful screen adaptations of Rodgers and Hammerstein's *Oklahoma!*, *The King and I*, and *South Pacific*, Lerner and Lowe's Oscar winning *Gigi*, an original modeled on their *My Fair Lady*, the Gershwins' *Porgy and Bess* (1959), and Bernstein and Sondheim's *West Side Story* (1961) inaugurated what we now call "the roadshow musical." These were musicals based on or imitative of Broadway hits; made at huge expense, they treated their sources with great reverence; they some-times cast movie stars whose voices had to be dubbed; and they were usually (but not always) exhibited at a single theatre once or twice a day in 70mm widescreen processes like Todd-AO, shown with overtures and intermissions, and charged higher than usual prices for seats needing to be reserved in advance. Following on the heels of these roadshows, and soon thereafter of the even more successful *My Fair Lady* (1964) and *The Sound of Music* (1965), these musicals tended to be nominated for many year-end awards, too. To be sure, many such roadshow musicals did not technically exhibit as roadshows but, like *The Music Man* (1962), *Gypsy* (1962), *Bye Bye Birdie* (1963), *The Unsinkable Molly Brown* (1964), and *Mary Poppins* (1964), opened on continuous showings at the prestigious Radio City Music Hall in New York

City. The roadshow musical subsequently made movie stars of Julie Andrews in *Mary Poppins* and *The Sound of Music* and Barbra Streisand in *Funny Girl* (1968).

The Sound of Music played extremely long runs on roadshow, showing for well over a year in small cities where several weeks would have been the norm for this type of attraction, and it inspired studios to go all out in producing expensive musicals for the rest of the decade. With the studio system now dismantled, the film companies, themselves subject to takeovers and mergers, tended to rely mostly on returns from a few expensive productions yearly to safeguard their bottom line. The spectacular success of MGM's *Ben-Hur* (1959) delayed the financial crisis that would later trouble that studio, causing its ownership to change hands and one of its backlots to be sold, and *The Sound of Music* rescued Fox from the dangers of bankruptcy due to the inflated budget and long production of *Cleopatra* (1963). Musicals like *The Sound of Music* thus seemed to promise instant success. At the end of 1968 five roadshow musicals competed for audiences in many US cities: *Funny Girl, Star, Finian's Rainbow, Chitty Chitty Bang Bang,* and *Oliver. Sweet Charity* (1969) premiered a few months later. The failure of all those expensive productions but *Funny Girl* (nominated for Oscar's best picture award) and *Oliver* (winning it) signaled the demise of roadshow musicals, although *Hello, Dolly!* (1969), *Goodbye Mr. Chips* (1969), *Paint Your Wagon* (1969), *Darling Lili* (1970), *On a Clear Day You Can See Forever* (1970), *Fiddler on the Roof* (1971), *1776* (1972), *Man of La Mancha* (1972), *Lost Horizon* (1973), and *Mame* (1974) were in the pipeline. Of these last musicals, only *Dolly* and *Fiddler* received nominations for best picture and had relatively long runs. The others all lost money.

By the 1970s, after the crushing failure of most of those big-budget extravaganzas the musical in its most recognizable form, once a signature genre and mainstay of the Hollywood movie factories, had lost its widespread appeal. During the 1970s and 1980s musical soundtracks on dramas, romantic comedies, and action films or in biopics and concert films effectively continued what had been the genre's once important cultural function of circulating popular music. Music videos, shown in the United States on the cable networks MTV and VH1, performed this role too.

With musicals no longer bankable and popular music itself dramatically different from Tin Pan Alley formats, the 1970s and 1980s were years of experimentation by some filmmakers and adherence to safe formulas by others. This was also the period in which the film industry was reinventing itself, artistically and economically, first during the late 1960s in the New Hollywood renaissance as the studios first changed hands, then in the mid-1970s and afterward as the enormous returns from *Jaws* (1975) and *Star Wars* (1977) encouraged the mentality of blockbuster tentpoles that still dominates today. Musicals were still being made during these years, to be sure. Returning to films after several triumphs onstage, Bob Fosse brought an innovative style of direction and editing to *Cabaret* (1972), an adaptation that revised its Broadway source while sustaining its theatricality, and *All That Jazz* (1979), an original with preexisting songs, both of which used numbers in new and different ways. *Cabaret* and *All That Jazz* deconstructed the genre's conventions of utopianism and authenticity, as did Herbert Ross's somewhat later *Pennies from Heaven* (1981).

Musicals also sought to reflect changes in popular music. *Tommy* (1975) and *Hair* (1979) each used a rock score. Robert Altman's *Nashville* (1975) pushed the musical form past its conventional limits with a large ensemble cast, some of whom wrote their own songs, a Country Western musical setting, and his improvisational style. In *Saturday Night Fever* (1977) director John Badham made cultural phenomena out of the disco sound, the Bee Gees soundtrack, and dancing star John Travolta. A streetwise kinetic energy likewise characterized the New York City teens' dancing and singing in Alan Parker's gritty, multiracial *Fame* (1980), an updating of the old Rooney-Garland "let's put on a show" teen musicals that was set at the New York High School for the Performing Arts. During the rest of the decade dance musicals drawing on contemporary tastes and attracting youth audiences, notably *Flashdance* (1983) and *Footloose* (1984), were popular hits with equally popular soundtrack albums. Prince electrified those same audiences with *Purple Rain* (1984), one of the few musicals of this time built around a black recording artist. However, the biggest hit of this period was the more traditional adaptation of the 1950s teen pastiche, *Grease* (1978) starring Travolta, which came out six months after *Saturday Night Fever* and which equaled *The Sound of Music* in its enormous popularity.

Mining much of that same young audience, *The Rocky Horror Picture Show* (1975), a gender bending musical spoof of the horror film, bombed in its initial theatrical runs; a year later it began to acquire a global cult following at weekend midnight shows that would last for the rest of the century and still continues in some locales today, making its costs back multiple times over. Audiences actively participated with the film while they watched—dressing in costumes, bringing props to match the dialogue, shouting some lines in unison, talking back to the characters at other points—and viewers went back repeatedly to see the film many times. Through fandom the participation "script" became standardized from coast to coast and in other countries.

Studios continued to adapt Broadway shows—*The Wiz* (1978), *Annie* (1982), *A Chorus Line* (1985)—and to try original musicals in a traditional form using big stars—*Funny Lady* (1975) and *A Star Is Born* (1976) with Barbra Streisand and *New York, New York* (1977) with Liza Minnelli. Biopics were more reliable: *Lady Sings the Blues* (1972), *The Buddy Holly Story* (1978), *Coal Miner's Daughter* (1980), *Sweet Dreams* (1985), *La Bamba* (1987), *What's Love Got to Do with It* (1993), and more recently, *Ray* (2004) and *Walk the Line* (2005). Biopics like these, as well as the fictionalized Janis Joplin biography, *The Rose* (1979), have always been ways to integrate music into a narrative without breaking the fourth wall; and just as the runaway success of *The Jolson Story* (1945) inspired musical biopics in the late 1940s and throughout the 1950s, so too the blockbuster success of *Funny Girl* with its star-making turn by Streisand, already a major recording artist and star of award-winning television specials before her film debut, may have prompted the musical biopic's revival in the early 1970s. Motown and Paramount tried for the same crossover stardom with Diana Ross in *Lady Sings the Blues* but had less success. After playing an adult version of Dorothy in Universal's *The Wiz*, Ross did not star again in theatrical movies, although her recording and concert career continued on fire.

What is interesting about biopics of this period is that they did not all embrace mainstream music and the people who rose to fame on the stage, radio, or film as in earlier decades with, say, *The Glenn Miller Story* (1954) and *The Benny Goodman Story* (1956), but dealt with African American and Latin performers (Billie Holiday in *Lady Sings the Blues*, Richie Valens in *La Bamba*, Ray Charles in *Ray*) and country western stars (Loretta Lynn in *Coal Miner's Daughter*, Pasty Kline in *Sweet Dreams*, Johnny Cash and June Carter in *Walk the Line*). Most of these biopics garnered high critical praise and Academy awards and nominations for the performances. These biopics, like the earlier ones, nonetheless had a nostalgic appeal because they looked back to music and singers from the past, which satisfied the nostalgia craze of this period. Trading on that nostalgia, MGM, no longer in the business of producing musicals or even distributing films by now, brought out compilations of numbers exploiting its halcyon past: *That's Entertainment!* (1974), *That's Entertainment, Part II* (1976), *That's Dancing!* (1985), and *That's Entertainment! III* (1994). A melding of dance and nostalgia, finally, made a giant hit of the dance musical set in a 1950s Jewish Catskills resort, *Dirty Dancing* (1987).

The traditional musical had always found a home in animation, so it is perhaps most fitting that animated features marked a return to that format. From *Snow White and the Seven Dwarfs* (1937) to *Sleeping Beauty* (1959), Walt Disney's animated features were mostly musicals with characters and animals singing and dancing to songs, many of which became standards. The so-called Disney Renaissance (1989–1999) began with the commercial and critical successes of the company's return to animated musicals: *The Little Mermaid* (1989), *Beauty and the Beast* (1991), *Aladdin* (1992), and *The Lion King* (1994). It is possible that, if a hipper and more jaded youth audience found it difficult to accept live actors breaking into song, cartoon characters doing so was more acceptable to them. The company's return to form with *Frozen* (2013), which rewrote Hans Christian Andersen's "The Snow Queen" to more resemble the blockbuster Broadway hit, *Wicked*, itself a revision of *The Wizard of Oz*, found a huge diverse audience of men and women, exceeding the young female demographic that was the core market for the film and all the merchandising associated with it.

BEAUTY AND THE BEAST (1991/2017)

The predominantly hand-drawn *Beauty and the Beast* was Disney's thirtieth animated feature; a work-in-progress version premiered at the New York Film Festival in late September, half a dozen weeks before the film's premiere in Hollywood, and the completed version was shown out of competition at the Cannes film festival the following spring. A critical and commercial success, *Beauty and the Beast* was the first animated feature to be nominated in the Best Picture category of the Academy Awards and the first to win the Golden Globe for Best Musical or Comedy. An IMAX version that included an additional number was released in 2002, a sing-along version opened for a limited run in 2010, and a 3D version came out in 2012. *Beauty and the Beast* spawned two direct-to-video sequels and a spin-off series on the Disney cable channel. As evidence of Disney's turn to the stage, a theatrical version using the full score with the addition of new songs opened on Broadway in 1994 and ran for thirteen years. Returning full circle, a live-action and CGI remake of the original came out in 2017, using the score from 1991 but eschewing the Broadway additions for several new tunes, and it was an enormous success globally, becoming (as of this writing) the second highest grossing musical of all time after *Frozen* (2013).

Figure 2.8 Belle (Paige O'Hara) sings the opening number in *Beauty and the Beast* (1991, Disney)

Figure 2.9 Lumiere (Jerry Orbach) invites Belle to "Be Our Guest" in *Beauty and the Beast* (1991, Disney)

The 1991 animated rendition is already structured to play like an integrated Broadway book musical, and it includes two stars of the Great White Way, Angela Lansbury voicing Mrs. Potts and Jerry Orbach voicing Lumiere. A prelude recounts the trans-formation of the prince, who is "spoiled, selfish, and unkind," into the temperamental, angry Beast (Robby Benson). Songs by Howard Ashman and Alan Menken mark character development and plot movement. The opening communal number, "Belle," establishes the heroine's (Paige O'Hara) outlier status in and sense of being constrained by the provincial village where she lives and her longing to live a more adventurous, fulfilling life; a reprise recounts her determination not to marry the boorish, narcissistic Gaston (Richard White). Complementing that first song, "Gaston" has the villagers celebrating Gaston's virility, the lyrics mocking his displays of aggressive manliness. After Belle agrees to remain in the Beast's castle in exchange for freeing her father, the enchanted servants—transformed into objects like a candlestick, clock, wardrobe, teapot—sing and dance to "Be Our Guest," turning Belle's dinner into an elaborate production number, with Lumiere evoking cabaret stars like Maurice Chevalier and overhead or angled shots of the ensemble quoting Busby Berkeley. Indeed, while Berkeley's camera work objectified his showgirls by visualizing them in abstract, kaleidoscopic patterns, "Be Our Guest" does the reverse. Here objects dance and sing like humans. Soon, Beauty and the Beast's relation thaws, first in the number "Something There," sung by the pair in voiceover, and then in the title tune, sung by Mrs. Potts, as the pair dine and then waltz, the camera swirling around them as they dance (this scene is the only one that made use of CGI technology). The Beast gives Belle her freedom because she misses her father. In the meantime, Gaston means to kill the beast, both for a trophy and because he senses Belle's affection for him, and in "The Mob Song" he riles the fearful villagers into going with him to attack the castle. Of course, the enchanted servants defeat the mob, a dejected and injured Beast defeats Gaston when he sees that Belle has returned to him, she acknowledges her love, and the spell is broken.

Figure 2.10 Belle (Emma Watson) sings the opening number in *Beauty and the Beast* (2017, Disney)

Figure 2.11 Lumiere (Ewan McGregor) and Cogworth (Ian McCellen) invite Belle to "Be Our Guest" in *Beauty and the Beast* (Disney, 2017)

The remake follows its animated source almost to the letter, including repeating many similar long shots of the village or countryside, this time enabled by developments in CGI. "Be Our Guest," moreover, mirrors the animated version but keeps upping the ante to do it one better in its eye-popping effects. In many respects the 2017 *Beauty and the Beast*, even with Emma Watson (Belle), Dan Stevens (Beast), Luke Evans (Gaston) and Kevin Kline (Maurice, Belle's father) in the lead roles, is another animated musical; the many castle scenes involving Lumiere (Ewen McGregor), Mrs. Potts (Emma Thompson), Cogworth the clock (Ian McCellen), Madame de Garderobe, the wardrobe (Audra MacDomnald), and Maestro Cadenza, the harpsicord (Stanley Tucci), are all achieved through computer animation. And compared with the humanoid features of the enchanted objects in 1991, here those same characters look more, well, hyperrealistic *as* objects.

Furthermore, whereas the *Beauty and the Beast* of 1991 runs a lean 85 minutes (the longer version with the restoration of the number "Human Again" runs 90 minutes), in 2017 it runs 129 minutes. A few new songs added to the original score extend the length. After "Belle," Maurice sings "How Can a Moment Last Forever," which becomes his theme; "Days in the Sun," begun with the Beast in flashback as a spoiled youth but extending to the present for Belle and the enchanted servants to sing, occurs after Belle runs away and the Beast rescues her from the wolves (which also happens in 1991); the Beast now has a solo, "Evermore," in which he recounts his resignation to Belle's departure after he sets her free to rescue her father. A finale is also added after the enchantment is reversed, with Audra MacDonald and Emma Thompson reprising the title song. Additionally, less juvenile humor replace the slapstick comedic bits from 1991 that link it to cartoons, scenes from the original have more dialogue, and more backstory is added, both to the Beast's past life (the prelude is longer, with MacDonald singing an aria, and an account of his upbringing is later noted) and to Belle's (she and the Beast take a magical trip to Paris where she learns about the fate of her mother, who died of plague, requiring Maurice to flee the contagion with his infant daughter). The enchanted rose, which signals the deadline looming over the Beast when his enchantment will be made permanent, becomes a motif threaded throughout.

Whereas one may argue that the 1991 *Beauty and the Beast* confirmed the return of the traditional musical, the huge returns of the 2017 version showed that a contemporary moviegoing audience still found the genre appealing a quarter of a century later. Some of that appeal no doubt has to do with nostalgia, for many of those adult viewers in 2017 had first seen the earlier one as children, whether in theatres or on home video; its success also owes something to the popularity of long-running Broadway spectaculars like the 1994 stage transfer. The two versions of *Beauty and the Beast* demonstrate what has become the Disney pipeline for its animated features, which now go from cinemas to the stage and back to the cinemas in an updated version that exploits new technology. As important, both renditions of *Beauty and the Beast* reflect the ongoing mutual relation of film musicals and the recording industry. In 1991, Céline Dion and Peabo Bryson sang the title song as the end titles rolled, their recording winning a Grammy and becoming a best-seller; as the end titles roll in 2017, Dion sings "How Does a Moment Last Forever," Josh Grobin performs "Evermore," and now Ariana Grande and John Legend do the title song.

In the early 1990s the Disney studio tried to revive the live-action musical, too, with *Newsies* (1991), which subsequently found a cult audience of teens and became a successful Broadway adaptation, and *Swing Kids* (1992), both starring a young Christian Bale. However, the critical and financial success of both *Moulin Rouge!* (2001) and *Chicago* (2002) saw live-action musicals come back in full force every year in the present century. Most have been adaptations of Broadway shows, and the results have been uneven. For every critical and box-office success—*Dreamgirls* (2006), *Hairspray* (2007), *Sweeney Todd, the Demon Barber of Fleet Street* (2007), *Mamma Mia* (2008), *Les Miserables* (2012), *Into the Woods* (2014)—there were duds that failed to capture the source's theatrical magic—*The Phantom of the Opera* (2004), *Rent* (2005), *The Producers* (2005), *Nine* (2009), *Rock of Ages* (2012). A few originals, such as *Across the Universe* (2007), which repurposed the Beatles catalogue, and *Burlesque* (2010), which paired Christina Aguilara with Cher, failed to catch on, as did remakes of *Footloose* (2011) and *Dirty Dancing* (2017).

Disney had better success with *Enchanted* (2007), a combination of animation and live-action that poked affectionate fun at its princess fairy tales, and the *High School Musical* trilogy, the first two of which appeared on its cable channel in 2006 and 2007 with the third going to theatres to capitalize on star Zac Efron's popularity. Acapella singing turned the *Pitch Perfect* trilogy (2012, 2015, 2017) into hits. Rap was introduced to the genre, first in *8 Mile* (2002) and then in the biopic about the group N.W.A., *Straight Out of Compton* (2015); both had their many admirers and stretched the genre, though they are usually categorized not as musicals but as "dramas with music." The same label, though, has also been applied to the newest remake of *A Star Is Born* (2018) with Lady Gaga and the biopic about Freddie Mercury, *Bohemian Rhapsody* (2018), possibly because in both cases all the numbers, and there are many, are show numbers. (But as I have argued in the previous chapter, this should not exclude such films from being considered musicals.) On the other hand, while its promotion shies away from advertising it as a full-fledged musical, the new Elton John biopic, *Rocketman* (2019), does not limit the music to a stage but fashions many of his songs into bona fide numbers featuring Taron Egerton, who portrays John, and other cast members singing and dancing in nontheatrical settings.

For all the peaks and valleys in its history, the Hollywood musical continues to thrive. The phenomenal success of *Frozen* is no exception but a confirmation. The Disney corporation, in fact, has transferred most of their lauded animated features from the 1990s to Broadway, and did so in 2018 with *Frozen* as well, and is now remaking their stage productions as live-action, CGI-enhanced musicals, the first being *Beauty and the Beast* (2017), with *Aladdin* (2019) and *The Lion King* (2019) coming out two years later, and *The Little Mermaid* in development. The traditional format still exhibits a resilient ability to adapt to changes in musical styles while remaining consistent with conventions from the past, and it is still be able to attract large audiences, especially as television renewed the genre's appeal with *High School Musical* on Disney's cable channel, musical series such as *Glee* (2009–2015), *Smash* (2012–2013), and *Crazy Ex-Girl Friend* (2015–2019), one-off musical episodes of popular series, such as *Buffy the Vampire Slayer*'s "Once More with Feeling" (2001), and live revivals of Broadway hits such as *The Sound of Music Live* on NBC in the United States in 2013 and on ITV in the United Kingdom on 2015.

New songwriters have come to prominence in both animated and live-action musicals as well: Alan Menkin and various lyricists, Marc Shaiman and Scott Wittman, Lynn Ahrens and Stephen Flaherty, Kristen Anderson-Lopez and Robert Lopez, Benj Paskin and Justin Paul. These songwriters balance writing for Hollywood and Broadway. And if there are contemporary directors identified with the genre they are Rob Marshall, who moved from stage to film with *Chicago* and has since done several musicals (*Nine* [2009], *Into the Woods* [2014], and *Mary Poppins Returns* [2018]), Adam Shankman (*Hairspray*, *Rock of Ages* [2011]), Kenny Ortega (*Newsies*, the *High School Musical* trilogy), and Bill Condon (*Dreamgirls*, the 2017 *Beauty and the Beast*). With recent musicals written directly for the screen—notably *La La Land* (2016) and *The Greatest Showman* (2017)—scoring high grosses, the film musical continues to serve as bankable product for Hollywood, albeit not on the same scale as some seventy or eighty years ago.

3

ANALYZING MUSICALS

Whether happening onscreen as stage performances or as spontaneous expressions of a character's emotions, numbers in a musical not only distinguish the genre but they are central to appreciating a given film's simplicity or its complexity. The narrative cannot be entirely discounted, to be sure, for it works with (or in some cases, against) the numbers to raise certain themes from which a film's meaning accrues. By the same token, films do not exist in isolation from the industry producing them and the society watching them, so the historical and cultural contexts are equally significant in understanding what and how musicals generate their meaning. This chapter will examine five different approaches that have dominated film scholarship and that can help us to see more closely how numbers work in musicals. Together, the five modes of close reading and analysis that I describe in this chapter—reading musicals for their utopian sensibility, for their transformation of mass art into folk art, for their dual focus structure, for their camp, for their historical density and intersectionality—reveal the genre's ideological preoccupations and hence the cultural work it has performed, particularly notable during its heyday when studios turned out musicals like clockwork. Each mode of analysis, moreover, addresses the problematic basis of musicals, namely, what the energy of performing musically signifies and how the genre formally channels this energy.

1 THE UTOPIAN SENSIBILITY OF MUSICALS

According to Richard Dyer, musicals, like other forms of popular entertainment, project a utopian sensibility, which is to say that their "utopianism is contained in the feelings [a musical] embodies. It presents, head-on as it were, what utopia would feel like rather than how it would be organized" (Dyer 2002: 20). He singles out five values that are embodied in the utopian feelings represented by numbers: *energy* as opposed to exhaustion; *abundance* as opposed to scarcity; *intensity* as opposed to dreariness; *transparency* as opposed to manipulation; and *community* as opposed to social fragmentation (2–23, 26).

Consider, for instance, how these utopian values characterize the numbers in MGM's *Meet Me in St. Louis* (1944) starring Judy Garland. Set in that city as the 1904 World's Fair is due to open, the film recounts a year in the life of the Smith family, beginning in the summer of 1903. Esther (Garland), a middle child and the main protagonist, crushes on the boy next door, John Truett (Tom Drake). The other major character is the youngest child, five-year old Tootie (Margaret O'Brien), who has a morbid imagination—her many dolls "die" of various diseases and have funerals in her backyard; some viewers find Tootie's unregulated spirit charming and funny while others find the character disturbing. A plot conflict does not occur until midway in the film. On Halloween night the father, Mr. Smith (Leon Ames), announces that he has been promoted at his law firm and the family will relocate to New York City at the end of the year.

Right away several numbers—the title song passed along from family member to family member in the opening sequence, the reprise immediately afterward sung by Esther and her older sister Rose (Lucille Bremmer), the partygoers singing and dancing to "Skip to My Lou," and the song that gathers the unhappy Smith family together after they learn of the future move to New York City, "You and I"—evoke a strong sense of community. That these numbers also show off their location in the Smiths' house at 5135 Kensington Avenue, a house teeming with material evidence of the family's comfortable life in every room, further associates them with bourgeois *abundance*. By comparison, Esther's solos, the pining "Boy Next Door" and mournful "Have Yourself a Merry Little Christmas," are notable for the *intensity* of Judy Garland's singing, just as Esther's overexcited rendition of "The Trolley Song" and "Under the Bamboo Tree," her song and dance duet with Tootie at the party, evoke Garland's high-spirited *energy* as a performer. Finally, Esther's "Over the Bannister," which she quietly sings on the stairs to the boy next door at the party's end shows a *transparency* of feelings, as more conventional love songs in musicals typically do.

Figure 3.1 Esther (Judy Garland) sings of "The Boy Next Door" in *Meet Me in St. Louis* (1944, MGM)

Admittedly, Dyer's terms are relative, the classification of numbers oftentimes open to further discussion and possibly even disagreement. I already noted that the *community* numbers also signify *abundance*. One could focus more on the lyrics of "The Boy Next Door" to argue that it represents *transparency*, as Esther reveals her longing for John Truett, or on how passengers sing along in "The Trolley Song" under Esther's direction to claim that this number represents *community*. Regardless, Dyer's point holds, namely, that in their lyrics, performances, choreography, settings and costumes, and musical arrangements, numbers (even sad songs of longing or heartbreak) entertain by evoking a utopian sense of liberation from everyday life and its restrictions. This utopian sense permeates every frame of *Meet Me in St. Louis*: in its spectacle (the production numbers), unmediated expressiveness (Garland's solos and the group dancing), and visual and sonic excess (the outdoor St. Louis street set and interiors of the Smith house, all built for this film at MGM under director Vincente Minnelli's command; the lush orchestrations and sophisticated musical arrangements and underscoring; and the supersaturated Technicolor palette).

To talk about the musical genre in this way according to Dyer is not to criticize it for being frivolous and escapist, but to acknowledge that its utopian sensibility satisfies wants that real life fails to address, even though, as he further points out, the feelings comprising this sensibility "point to gaps or inadequacies in capitalism, but only those gaps or inadequacies that capitalism proposes itself to deal with." In other words, as an industrial product manufactured to make a profit, a musical "provides alternatives *to* capitalism which will be provided *by* capitalism" (Dyer 2002: 27, emphasis in original). From this perspective, what makes numbers impossible in terms of the feelings they orchestrate is precisely what makes them most appealing and possibly disruptive of capitalist ideology since they project communal and individual desires that can never be realized as fully or as clearly offscreen.

Still, while numbers exert pressure on the realistic coherence and illusionism of the surrounding narrative, the reverse holds true as well, for a realistically grounded narrative can put pressure on the numbers' utopian sensibility, thereby taming or resisting it. Although it takes a while (not until we have heard six of the film's eight songs) to occur, the turn-of-the-twentieth-century narrative of *Meet Me in St. Louis* challenges the utopian spirit of the Smith household once Mr. Smith (Leon Ames) announces that the family must move to New York. His family's hostile reaction establishes him as a patriarch exerting authority over a feminine household. With the one son away at college, the Smith household is otherwise dominated by women—Mrs. Smith (Mary Astor), her four daughters, and the servant Katie (Marjorie Main). Even Grandpa Prophater may be from the matriarchal line given his surname. The opening sequence of *Meet Me in St. Louis* pivots around everyone but Mr. Smith knowing why dinner is being served an hour earlier (so that Rose can take the long-distance phone call from her beau and hopefully receive his marriage proposal) indicating, as he himself complains, the father's status as an outsider to his own family. Before dinner, too, he stops Esther and Rose's singing of the title song—an ominous gesture in a musical!

To be sure, one number, "You and I," reconciles the family with Mr. Smith as they join in the singing, resigned to his authority in mandating the move to New York City, while another number causes him to change his mind when he overhears Esther singing "Have Yourself a Merry Little Christmas" to Tootie and watches his hysterical youngest child rush outside to destroy her snow people so that no one else can have them. However, the narrative's configuration of the Smith women shows their inevitable containment by patriarchal culture—or as Esther states, as she dresses for the Christmas Eve dance, by her necessary and first time "corseting" to engage men there as an attractive young woman.

With the unlawful, uncensorable, and delightfully morbid five-year-old Tootie as a starting point, each female in the Smith family moves closer toward the calm but repressed temperament of their mother, who wields power because she knows how to handle her husband but can only do so in the space of her home. As Dyer puts it in an essay on this musical, a sense of sadness colors *Meet Me in St. Louis* "partly from a

Figure 3.2 Esther (Judy Garland) comforts Tootie who wants to kill her snow people rather than leave them when the family moves to New York in *Meet Me in St. Louis* (1944, MGM)

recognition that Tootie's—all children's, everyone's—energies are terrible, that the price we pay for order, stability, security, and civilization is the loss of the excitement, vigour and desire that left untrammeled would destroy us" (Dyer 2012: 79).

Registering this sadness, the female characters form a continuum with Esther in the pivot position, no longer a child like Tootie but not yet the full-fledged adult like her sister Rose or her mother. Esther's demure behavior with John Truett at the party is a self-conscious pose of female gentility; later, she impulsively hits and bruises him when she mistakenly thinks he harmed Tootie on Halloween night. Furthermore, in the family Esther has the central "role of facilitating harmony" and "the interactions of others" since she negotiates the many family squabbles or crises that pepper the story (Dyer 2012: 69). The oldest

Smith daughter, Rose, is herself already adept at flirting with potential suitors, while the second to youngest, Agnes, shares Tootie's spirit of unlawful riotousness, as evident in the Halloween sequence, but, as also shown there, Agnes is already more socialized and hence somewhat more regulated. (She dresses as a ghoulish woman whereas Tootie dresses as a ghoulish man.) From this perspective, the narrative of *Meet Me in St Louis*, set against the utopian liberation of Esther's numbers, revolves around her place as a young female secure in her home but about to leave it when she marries John Truett, which will force her to tamp down on her energy, intensity, and transparency (all evident in the numbers), much as her mother and Rose have done and as Agnes and even Tootie will eventually do as well. The alternative would be for Esther to become like the unmarried live-in servant, Katie. The utopian numbers push against that inevitability.

2 MASS ART AS FOLK ART

"The Hollywood musical," Jane Feuer writes in her book with that title, "as a genre perceives the gap between producer and consumer, the breakdown of community designated by the very distinction between performer and audience, as a form of original sin" (Feuer 1993: 3). A motion picture, produced in an industrial setting and reliant on various technologies for filming and exhibition, is aimed at a mass audience; the screen itself symbolizes the separation in time and space of the film's production from its consumption. Musicals demand a lot of behind the scenes labor before scenes and numbers are shot, during shooting, and in the editing room afterward, so they never capture a performance unmediated and in raw form. Folk art, by comparison, was created by entertainers—musicians, singers, storytellers, dancers—who interacted more directly with their audience; the folk audience kept its art—songs, poetry, sagas— in circulation through its repetition, while also adding to, subtracting from, or reimagining it. This is one reason much folk art from long ago is authorless. The convention of filming numbers (at least until recently) with few edits, long takes, and direct address means to simulate the experience of live or "folk" entertainment as captured on celluloid; however, the convention of prerecording songs and dance music, the fact that numbers are edited from numerous takes, and the manipulation of the camera's position as it moves in and out of space during filming of numbers, all of this should nevertheless remind us that a musical is a product of industrial engineering and technological interventions.

According to Feuer, the musical genre traditionally closes the breach between filmed and live entertainment, turning the fact of its being a mass art into a semblance of folk art, through a "process of creation and cancellation" (13). Musicals cancel their own engineering through prop numbers—a character dancing with a mop (Gene Kelly in *Thousands Cheer* [1944]) or coatrack (Fred Astaire in *Royal Wedding* [1951]) or a dog (Eleanor Powell in *Lady Be Good* [1941]), say, instead of a human partner. Borrowing from anthropology, Feuer calls this convention "bricolage." Bricolage means "tinkering" or making do with materials at hand by finding new uses for them, as when one repurposes something. In musicals the bricolage number creates an effect of spontaneity; it effaces in the onscreen representation all the calculation that went into its own production.

Additionally, by presenting as rehearsals or auditions or some other kind of extemporaneous performance finished numbers that likewise require much behind-the-scenes work in their planning and practicing, musicals further efface what was carefully staged and choreographed in order to give the impression that "dancing is utterly natural and that dancing is easy" (9). The same happens with singing when a character performs off the cuff yet wows her listeners at a party or an audition, as Esther and Tootie do in "Under the Bamboo Tree." This convention of masking choreography and rehearsing blurs the difference between an entertainer's being a professional, one who performs for payment, and an amateur, who entertains just for the love of it but is real good at it nonetheless. This is one reason why the style of singing in musicals has tended toward naturalism in terms of how the voice registers on film.

Eliminating or rejecting "the more exploitative aspects of profession-alism," musicals show how "singing and dancing may emerge from the joys of ordinary life" (14).

Musicals further create an impression of being folk art through the community they imagine on and off the stage. The convention of direct address offers one way of giving the appearance of unmediated connection between performer and offscreen audience. Similarly, the singalong song or the passed-along song (when one character passes a song to another character who passes it along to a third) is a way of grounding a musical's entertainment value in an off-stage community. In the opening of Meet Me in St. Louis, as noted earlier, one member of the Smith family sings the title song, encounters another person in the household, who continues the song, passes it on to another person, and so on, establishing the family's amateur musicality.

Still another way that musicals work to associate their entertainment with folk art is in terms of how they use space. Backstage musicals tend to break down how the proscenium stage may be perceived as a bar-rier between performers and the onscreen (and hence offscreen) audi-ence, suggesting that the stage is the world, while musicals not about putting on a show tend to reimagine a proscenium "out of ordinary space," suggesting that the world is a stage, as when Esther Smith sings "The Boy Next Door," framed by a big picture window (24). Theatrical stages are there to be cancelled, in short, their distance bridged, yet any nontheatrical space can become a stage, bridging the distance between performer and audience in another way. Finally, especially in self-reflexive musicals that peel the protective layer off their own tech-nology, the process of demystifying the protocols of producing enter-tainment is always followed by the remystification of the Hollywood musical itself as pure entertainment (42–47).

Feuer illustrates her claims primarily by citing musicals from MGM and the Freed unit, but musicals from other studios could serve her purpose equally well. Consider Paramount's Holiday Inn (1942) starring Bing Crosby and Fred Astaire. At the film's start Jim Hardy (Cosby) and Ted Hanover (Astaire) are teamed in a singing-dancing nightclub act with and are also romantic rivals for Lila Dixon (Virginia Dale), who is engaged to Jim but in love with both men. Tired of performing, Jim retires to a farm in Connecticut while Lila, not wanting to forsake the limelight, jilts Jim and continues to perform with Ted, her new fiancée. Bored on his farm but not wanting the grind of working nightclubs year-round, Ted turns his farm into a night club open only on holidays. In the meantime, Lila leaves Ted for a Texas millionaire, so Ted wants Linda Mason (Marjorie Reynolds), Jim's new performing partner at his Holiday Inn and his new love interest, to go to Hollywood with him. The narrative, in sum, sets up the contest between Jim, his leisurely performing, and the country setting of Holiday Inn, on the one hand, and Ted, his professional ambitions, and the urban nightspots and Hollywood studio where he performs, on the other. Crosby's first solo as Jim, in fact, is "Lazy," sung over a montage of his misadventures as a farmer, which inspire him to turn his farm into an inn that will be open only fifteen times a year, thus reconciling his talent with his dislike of working hard. The film's many musical numbers then delineate the Jim/Ted opposition, as Feuer's template helps to highlight.

The two polished show numbers in New York nightclubs (Jim, Ted, and Lila's "I'll Capture Your Heart Singing" and Ted and Lila's "You're Easy to Dance With"), as well as the montage of Ted and Linda dancing while making a movie in Hollywood, contrast with Jim and Linda's looser, more impromptu numbers happening at Holiday Inn ("White Christmas," "Come to the Holiday Inn/Happy Holidays," "One Minute to Midnight," etc.). It is unclear, in fact, how many people work at the inn since Jim cannot pay his employers at first and expects them to share in the profits, if there are any, yet he has servers, a full orchestra, and at times backup singers and dancers. When Hollywood comes a-calling, wanting to use Holiday Inn as a subject for filming, Jim at first refuses because he had only wanted "a single little layout where we do our best at the work we know without having any illusions of glory." Linda herself wants to perform yet when introducing herself to Jim she says, "I can sing a little and dance." While performing at the inn she still lives in New York, where she works at a flower shop to support herself.

Figure 3.3 Jim (Bing Crosby) sings "White Christmas" to Linda (Marjorie Reynolds) in *Holiday Inn* (1942)

The singing and dancing at Holiday Inn occur without much rehearsing and with impromptu choreography. After Lila leaves him, a highly inebriated Ted arrives at Holiday Inn and dances with Linda to a reprise of "You're Easy to Dance With" but in a (obviously painstakingly choreographed) slapdash manner; the other patrons leave the dance floor to watch and applaud wildly at the number's finish. Ted has found a replacement for Lila but was too drunk to remember who she is, and his agent (Walter Abel) only saw her from the back. On Lincoln's birthday, although "Abraham" has been costumed and rehearsed, at the last minute Jim turns it into a full blackface number with apparently new staging and costumes in order to hide Linda from Ted. Then on Valentine's Day Linda arrives an hour before opening and mentions that she and Jim haven't even rehearsed their numbers yet. He sings "Be Careful It's My Heart," a song he wrote especially for her.

Ted unexpectedly arrives and draws Linda into a dance to the song's melody, and the seeming spontaneity of their graceful movement likewise belies the choreography and rehearsal that obviously went into creating this number. Because Ted then decides to join the company at the inn with a scheme of wooing Linda for himself, on Washington's Birthday Jim, working as the bandleader, keeps changing the speed and style of their music as they dance to "I Can't Tell a Lie." The couple, in eighteenth-century costume, have to keep adjusting their dancing to match the rapid shifts in tempo back and from waltz to swing (and even at one point, to the conga!) every time Linda gets too close to Ted for Jim's comfort.

Bricolage comes into play with Ted's exuberant dancing with firecrackers on Independence Day. With Jim having shanghaied Linda so that she cannot perform with Ted before the Hollywood people who have come to watch them, Ted has to invent a new solo dance on the spot; grabbing handfuls of firecrackers and stuffing them in his pockets, as he dances to "Let's Say It with Firecrackers," he tosses out one explosive sparkler after another in time with his intricate footwork. The opposite of bricolage is engineering. Late in the film, after Linda and Ted have gone to Hollywood to make the Holiday Inn film, on Thanksgiving and with the inn no longer open, an unhappy Jim listens to a recording of his singing "I've Got Plenty to be Thankful For." The cheerful number is at odds with Jim's desolate mood, so the context of his listening to it in the empty inn undercuts the mass produced sincerity of the recording, which is an obvious work of engineering removed from the supposedly more authentic emotion we see the singer enacting on screen as he listens.

The setting of the inn itself brings these various threads together to epitomize folk art. Originally a farmhouse, the open space of the club area functions as a proscenium stage for the numbers. As the film progresses and possibly due to the inn's success, the performance space even seems to increase in size, just as backup chorus and dancers become more visible, as on Independence Day. On this holiday the show moves outside, enabling the performing space to get even larger and more expansive while emphasizing its natural setting. In contrast with the earlier nightclub performances, moreover, the audience at the inn becomes part of the community. On New Year's Eve, Jim and Linda mingle with the crowd while singing, and before drunken Ted arrives, the patrons dance to the music, with one drunken lady grabbing Jim for a dance much as Ted will engage Linda shortly thereafter.

Finally, when Jim travels to Hollywood to ask Linda to return to him, the film's self-reflexively turns on itself. The Hollywood set is an exact reproduction of the inn: "One of the most authentic jobs we've ever done," someone tells Jim when he arrives at the studio in Hollywood. A long shot shows Hollywood's replica of the inn inside a large soundstage along with all the engineering (the camera, sound boom, lights) and manual labor (the crew bustling about to prepare for the shoot) necessary for filming, including a playback for Linda's number to be filmed there, a reprise of "White Christmas." That the reproduction in "Hollywood" and Jim's original in "Connecticut" are indistinguishable from each other momentarily punctures the film's own illusionism, revealing the engineering and mass production that manufacture folk values in the movies. This demystification may send us back to earlier points in the film, as when Jim and Linda travel in a horse-drawn carriage from church back to the inn on Easter Sunday as he sings, "Easter Parade." The obviously painted backdrop of the outdoor scene here records how the number was likewise filmed on a soundstage.

Holiday Inn then remystifies itself as the source of pure "folk" entertainment when it concludes once again at the inn in Connecticut on New Year's Eve, now with two couples, Jim and Linda and Ted and Lila, performing a reprise of "I'll Capture Your Heart." The final shot is of the inn's exterior, mirroring the Hollywood version exactly but without the latter's imagery of industrial engineering in order to remystify the inn's "folk" value as entertainment done for the pleasure of it and not, as Jim said, "for the glory." Nor for the professional ambition and monetary gains, for that matter, which were Ted and Lila's motives, and Paramount's too in making this film.

Figure 3.4 Hollywood's reproduction of the inn in *Holiday Inn* (1942, Paramount)

In its setting as well as its numbers *Holiday Inn* performs the leger-demain of transforming the Hollywood film musical into folk art that effaces its identity as an entertainment industrially produced to be consumed by a mass audience. This has the effect of appearing to close the gap in time and space between the moment of the musical's pro-duction at Paramount studios and its consumption later on in movie theaters. Feuer's template enables us to see more clearly how *Holiday Inn* detaches the training, rehearsals, backstage labor, and professionalism of entertainment by relocating it from the city to the country; the film can then reattach connotations of "live" entertainment—spontaneous and unrehearsed singing and dancing—to the many numbers occurring at Holiday Inn.

In working toward this end, though, a residual and not inconse-quential effect is the film's suturing of the spectator to the numbers' ideological content, their celebration of Americanness through national holidays, which nostalgically evoke a conservative view of American entertainment. These folk values would have been very current and comforting to the nation when the film was released, about ten months after Pearl Harbor and the United States' entrance into World War II. By the same token, the numbers and their folk connotations of Americana are embedded in heterosexual romance and the men's rivalry over the women.

Too, the folk values of Holiday Inn naturalize the blackface number, "Abraham," just as Jim's African American servant, Mamie (Louise Beavers), and her two children are themselves characterized as simple "folk" who speak not in proper English but in "black" dialect. While in the kitchen during "Abraham," the film cuts to Mamie singing the lyrics as call and response with the children, although the onscreen audience do not hear them. She works for Jim as his only constant employee from the time he arrives at the farm, and she is the one who tells Jim to travel to Hollywood to tell Linda that he loves her. The whiteness of the film's numbers is at least implicitly built upon the black servant's labor in the kitchen, which is visible to viewers if never commented on by the patrons of Holiday Inn, just as her "amateur" singing talent is bracketed from the performance space and her character motivates the primary couple's reunion.

3 THE DUAL-FOCUS STRUCTURE

In his extensive anatomy of the musical in its three subgenres—the show musical, the fairy tale musical, and the folk musical—Rick Altman argues that the genre organizes meanings through the central male/female couple. The couple represents mutually exclusive values, such as masculine/feminine, mature/youthful, city/country, riches/beauty, aristocratic/bourgeois, work/entertainment, boredom/excitement, dream/reality, and so on. Formally, the musical parallels the lovers through a dual focus structure with comparable numbers, scenes, feelings, motifs, locations, and so forth that delineate their opposition yet anticipate their comparability:

> Once we have understood the dual-focus approach we easily grasp the importance of the many set pieces or production numbers which some see as cluttering the musical's program and interrupting its plot. The plot, we now recognize has little importance to begin with; the oppositions developed in the seemingly gratuitous song-and-dance number, however, are instrumental in establishing the structure and meaning of the film.

> (Altman 1989: 27)

Altman's point is that while the couple's successful formation by the musical's closure happily resolves their paralleled differences as man and woman, "a secondary but essential opposition [arises] alongside the primary sexual division: each sex is identified with a particular attitude, value, desire, location, age, or other characteristic attribute. These secondary attributes always begin diametrically opposed and mutually exclusive" (24). This secondary opposition is less easily harmonized, especially if referring to the real social world outside musicals, although the genre tries to give every impression of harmonizing them through the couple's ultimate union. The united couple represent the joining together of irreconcilable oppositions—after all, by definition an opposition like mature/youthful, city/country, or riches/beauty is irreconcilable. For this reason, Altman concludes that musicals function as "a cultural problem-solving device":

> By recognizing terms previously seen as mutually exclusive, the musical succeeds in reducing an unsatisfactory paradox to a more workable configuration, a concordance of opposites. Traditionally, this is the function which society assigns to myth. Indeed we will not be far off the mark if we consider that the musical fashions a myth out of the American courtship ritual.

> (27)

Altman's dual-focus template most precisely applies to the fairy tale subgenre, as I shall show in a moment, but it extends as well to the other two subgenres. "In the musical," he claims, "*the couple is the plot*" (35; Altman's emphasis). Thus in the show musical the equivalence of the couple and the show allows one side of the equation to work out (or give the impression of working out) the oppositions defining the other side. A folk musical like *Meet Me in St. Louis*, by contrast, tends to feature a spectrum of couples which allows the central couple's success to radiate outward to the community as an ameliorating force of unity and cohesion, thereby reconciling the secondary oppositions organized by the male/female dualism. Accordingly, this film ends with the three eldest Smith children happily coupled and, with their parents, grandparent, and two younger siblings, all attending the World's Fair together.

RKO's *Top Hat* (1935) starring Astaire in his more usual role as a film's sole romantic lead and Ginger Rogers, classified as a fairy tale musical in Altman's book, is an excellent example of how the dual focus works. The term "fairy tale" need not be taken literally for the subgenre gets its name from an exotic, dream-like setting, a plot driven by mistaken identities or disguises, and the basis of courtship in sexual desiring which is musicalized as a form of enchantment through song and dance.

In *Top Hat* Jerry Travers (Astaire), an entertainer, falls in love with Dale Tremont (Rodgers), who wears fashions designed by her patron, Albert Beddini (Erik Rhodes) as a means of inspiring wealthy customers to buy his gowns. She warms to Jerry but mistakenly assumes he is the husband of her best friend, Madge Hardwick (Helen Broderick). The real husband, Horace Hardwick (Edward Everett Horton), is Jerry's producer and close friend. Vacationing in Venice, Madge wants Jerry and Dale to meet, not knowing they have met already in the London hotel where they are each staying and invites both to join her. Still thinking that Jerry is Horace and determined not to submit to her attraction to him, Dale agrees to marry Beddini, though the marriage is never consummated and indeed not a legal union it turns out since the curate performing it was Bates (Eric Blore), Horace's valet, in disguise. Once the mistakes are cleared up, the right couple can finally be formed. The five numbers in *Top Hat* delineate the stakes of the couple's formation by dually focusing the film through the two leads and conveying their importance for the musical as a couple through dance. In other words, when viewed through its dual focus, *Top Hat* well illustrates how dancing works as a metaphoric expression of the couple's sexual desire and its consummation.

Top Hat opens in the all-male Thackeray Club where Jerry waits for Horace's arrival. The club members here are, like Horace, fussy middle-aged gentlemen. Confronted by the "no noise" policy, Jerry beats a rhythmic percussion solo with his feet as he leaves, identifying his character with noise, youthfulness, and unruliness. His defiance in leaving the club sets up the conditions for the first number, "No Strings (I'm Fancy Free)." Residing in Horace's fashionable London hotel suite, Jerry explains to his friend that he does not plan to get married and settle down. To illustrate, he sings that he has "No Strings," and to show he is "fancy free," he taps loudly throughout the hotel suite. His tapping prevents Dale from falling asleep in the room directly below. The camera's traveling from one floor down to the next, with Jerry dancing in his room and Dale in her bed immediately beneath him, is a visual sexual joke. Jerry retracts his determination to have "no strings" when Dale goes upstairs to complain and he immediately falls for her. Pouring sand on the floor from a standing ash tray and saying he will be Dale's sand man, Jerry lulls her to sleep with a gentle soft shoe dance to a reprise of "No Strings."

This first number establishes Jerry and Dale as the central couple through their opposition. If Jerry stands for noise, energy, and dancing, then Dale stands for quiet, stillness, and repose. She is more domesticated than he, but he is more dynamic. Jerry's softening of his dancing to lull Dale back to sleep predicts how dance can reconcile their differences. This happens in the second number when Jerry's dancing seduces Dale. Jerry sings "Isn't This a Lovely Day (To Be Caught in the Rain)?" to calm her fear of thunder and draws her into a challenge tap dance. Here the choreography has Astaire and Rogers matching each other's movement, step for step, regardless of which dancer initiates a challenging move and which one then performs the same dance steps equally well. This is not a dance that choreographs the different roles of man and woman, as ballroom dancing does; rather, if he twirls her around, she does the same to him. The dancing here establishes their parity in the sexual game, and it is the means by which Dale falls in love with Jerry. However, the next morning Dale confusedly thinks Jerry is Horace so she flees with Beddini to stay with Madge in Venice.

In contrast with the other characters, Jerry and Dale are both youthful Americans; more to the point, as "Lovely Day" shows, they are both musical, which will prove to be the basis of their compatibility. They share another, more problematic commonality, though, which their union will implicitly resolve or banish in the manner of a fairy tale. Jerry and Dare are ex-patriot Americans who are residing in London

Figure 3.5 Jerry (Fred Astaire) and Dale (Ginger Rogers) dance to "Isn't it a Lovely Day" in *Top Hat* (1935, RKO)

during the Depression and living well by virtue of a rich employer, which accounts for their residence in luxurious hotel suites. Workers at the hotel suspect that Dale is Beddini's mistress, Horace thinks she is a gold digger seeking to entrap Jerry, and Dale assumes Jerry is Madge's husband so that his attentions are adulterous. Furthermore, just as Dale needs to appreciate Jerry's footwork as music and not noise, his persistence in pursuing her, like his violation of the Thackery club's silence and his indifference to the time of night or other hotel guests when dancing to "No Strings," indicates an ungovernable, undomesticated masculinity that needs to be reined in for his romance with Dale to succeed. This is the basis of the dual focus.

The third number, "Top Hat, White Tie, and Tails," is a show number meant to epitomize the opening night of Horace's musical production starring Jerry. This also occurs at the point when Jerry is confused by Dale's turnaround after their dancing to "Lovely Day"; all he knows is that she has slapped his face without cause and fled to parts unknown, so he may never see her again. Backed by an all-male dancing ensemble, Jerry performs the number in Astaire's signature costume of top hat, tails, and cane. While the lyrics characterize the singer as debonair, elegant, aristocratic, the staging renders his aggressive and angry masculinity as a dance, the choreography emphasizing the percussive beats of the star's tap shoes and cane hitting the dance floor in perfect rhythm. The number concludes with Jerry using his cane as a rifle to pick off the other dancers one by one like wooden ducks in a shooting gallery. "Top Hat" vacillates between, on one hand, masculinizing Jerry through his aggression and anger so that his energy as a dancer, in contrast with the effete other male characters in the film (Horace, Beddini, and Bates), stands out as a force threatening to romance, and on the other, confirming how male aggression and anger can be made orderly and tamed *as* choreography. Jerry is performing a performance of that masculinity which is highlighted as such by his show number.

When Jerry discovers Dale has fled to Venice to avoid him, he and Horace travel there for the weekend immediately after opening night. Confused by Madge's encouragement to spend time with Jerry, since she thinks he is Madge's husband while all Madge wants is to make a match of the younger couple, Dale reluctantly agrees to dance with Jerry. "If Madge doesn't care, then I certainly don't," she states and goes with him onto the dance floor. "Cheek to Cheek" is the most heterosexual number in *Top Hat*. Roger's costume, a satin gown adorned with ostrich feathers on the neck and shoulders and from the hips to the full-length skirt, contrasts with the unisex riding uniform she wore in "Lovely Day." In its narrative context, furthermore, the number is about illicitly dancing cheek to cheek since in Dale's mind the relation is adulterous because she thinks her partner is married to her best friend.

"Cheek to Cheek" is a waltz, with Astaire leading and Rogers following. They do a lot of side-by-side dancing with their intricate movement perfectly synchronized but the choreography also features her at several points doing a swooning, swaying backbend while in his arms, and the number reaches its highpoint with him twirling and lifting her off the ground several times until she falls into one more graceful backbend as she capitulates to his seductive charms. The number finishes with them waltzing cheek to cheek to the end of the terrace where they have been dancing. They lean against the enclosure and gaze at each other. The staging is intensely sexual as the waltz metaphorically enacts and climaxes Jerry's and Dale's mutual sexual desire. If there is any doubt, at the number's finish each dancer looks breathless yet satisfied, as they stand in repose as if they have orgasmed. All they need is the conventional postcoital cigarette (Astaire offers one to Rogers after they dance to "Night and Day" in *The Gay Divorcee* [1934]). "Cheek to Cheek" defines the couple's mutual attraction as intensely romantic and in doing so it brackets the couple's sexuality from the comedy occasioned by the other characters that surround them in the narrative. But the plot deriving from mistaken identities contextually signifies this sexuality as illicit, indicating a need to legitimate it socially through marriage.

The couple's social legitimation occurs through the fifth and final number, "The Piccolino," which happens after Jerry discloses his

Figure 3.6 Jerry (Fred Astaire) and Dale (Ginger Rogers) in the afterglow of dancing "Cheek to Cheek" in *Top Hat* (1935, RKO)

identity to Dale, though before Bates reveals that her marriage to Beddini was fraudulent. "The Piccolino" is a named-dance song. In the first segment thirty or more identically dressed couples dance to the music. In the second Dale sings the lyrics, after which an offscreen chorus repeats the song as the dancers continue their variations. In the third section Dale and Jerry go down to the dance floor. The camera focuses on their dancing feet, eventually moving to a full shot of them dancing in front of the ensemble who stand and watch in still formation. In contrast to the line dancing in the first two sections, where the choreography emphasized how the dance distinguished males and females, Dale and Jerry again dance in perfect sync, one matching the other's steps, posture, and hand movements, and each smiling broadly throughout. They dance off the floor and return to their table, toasting each other with champagne glasses as they sit down.

"The Piccolino" celebrates the two as a couple in a public setting that sets them apart from the ensemble of dancers. After all the mistaken identities are sorted out and Jerry and Dale are free to marry, Top Hat concludes with a reprise of this number as the couple dance together offscreen (and presumably back to London since Jerry has to resume performing in his new show). The ending rhymes with the opening titles, which lists the names of stars Astaire and Rodgers over footage of their legs and feet dancing to strains of "The Piccolino." That opening immediately established the dual focus, equated the dually-focused couple with dance, and posited dance as the basis of their union. The ending puts the period at the end of that opening sentence, so to speak.

Altman's template most fittingly applies to the classical musical produced by the studios in the 1930s, 1940s, and 1950s, and it helps to account for why romance plots seem intrinsic to musicals. It applies less well to musicals afterward, which problematize the dual focus even if reiterating it by concentrating on a heterosexual couple, or which eschew either a romance plot or a heterosexual couple. But one can already find the template straining to make sense of some classic musicals that focus on two male leads. For instance, one could read Holiday Inn through the dual focus of Jim and Linda but that would then discount the importance to the film of Ted even though Astaire has second star billing; and as I have already implied Holiday Inn builds a more complicated dual focus through Ted and Jim, who are buddies but not a couple. And while one may be tempted to view Meet Me in St. Louis through Esther and John, especially since the film's narrative is in part about forming couples among the young people, it always strikes me that it is more interesting to think about how this musical is focused dually through Esther and Tootie, who share an intimacy in their numbers and scenes together that reveals their bond and their differences in terms of their regulated and tempestuous energies. For that matter, integrated musicals lend themselves differently to a dual focus analysis than do aggregate musicals, especially when one star alone or specialty acts perform the numbers. Coney Island (1943) has a dual focus organized around Betty Grable and George Montgomery's characters but, since one star sings and the other doesn't, one side of the dual focus (Grable) works through her numbers and one side of it (Montgomery) works around them, which puts more emphasis on the narrative for his character as the film sets up the opposing values that the couple represents and ultimately reconcile.

Altman's template is nonetheless important as a means of calling attention to how musicals are, when all else is said and done, organized around and structured through numbers. I have intentionally dwelled primarily on the five numbers in *Top Hat* and left out much narrative misunderstandings involving the comic characters who do not sing or dance in order to show how, as flagship moments in this film, the numbers are the pivot points. They are the highlights not only for their magic as performances but also because of how they highlight the major turns in and musicalize the emotional depth of the characters' romance. But despite its utility, the dual-focus template is also heterocentric in its presumptions of value as organized through a sexually differentiated couple.

Altman subsequently modified his approach to recognize the limitations of that bias. Recognizing, as others after him had pointed out, the "extraordinary proportion of musicals [that] commence not with the heterosexual couple that occupies the text's later portions, but with one or more homosocial pairs," he identifies a generic tracing of "a very specific rite of passage," one putting aside same sex relationships, however innocent, "in favor of the heterosexual relationships that dominate musical endings" (Altman 2010: 25, 27–28). His modification identifies a variation of the ideological project undertaken by the classical musical (and other classical genres, too, for that matter), namely, its recounting of the socialization and maturation of adult heteromasculinity but this still tilts musicals in the direction of a dominant narrative of characters' progressing into heteronormativity. That may be consistent with the ideology governing the production of musicals, indeed of mainstream entertainment today as well as yesterday, but is that necessarily what audiences take from musicals and what filmmakers put in them, if only at the margins of those many standard heteronormative narratives that compose the genre?

4 CAMP AFFECT, STYLE, AND RECEPTION

Musicals have always had a strong and visible gay following. As Brett Farmer has observed, "In gay subcultural argot, the term *musical* has long been used as a coded reference to homosexuality; to describe someone as 'musical' or 'into musicals' is to describe them as homosexual" (Farmer 2000: 74). This loyal following makes a good deal of sense when one considers the labor force producing musicals and the over-the-top visual style that characterizes them.

A large number of gay, lesbian, and bisexual people worked on musicals behind the scenes as writers, directors, choreographers, composers, set dressers and designers, costumers, and so forth. Another, more pejorative popular nickname for the Arthur Freed unit within the film at the industry at the time was "Freed's fairies" because of the many gay people who worked in his production unit. Many of those same people also worked on musicals produced at this studio by other men, though the nickname adhered to Freed's unit because it was a tight, close-knit group who socialized together as well as worked together. By no means was MGM alone in offering a haven for artists of all nonconformist stripes working on motion pictures during this period.

To be sure, in the 1930s and 1940s terms like "gay," "bisexual,' "lesbian," and "homosexual" were not as rigidly fixed to identities (as opposed to partner choice) as they would be in subsequent decades when a stricter hetero/homosexual binary took hold as the dominant ideology, a way of thinking about sexual dissidence that has been succeeded by the more fluid understanding of the relation of gender to sexed bodies and both to sexual desiring that has become more prevalent today among Millennials and Generation Zers. In any event, despite their own self-identification and even marital status at the time, that many queer people worked at all the studios alongside straight men and women on musicals, a genre encouraging, even requiring an over-the-top imagination when planning numbers and designing sets and costumes, helps to explain a visible camp style that offers alternative positions for viewing musicals.

What make a style legible as "camp"? This is a complex question and the answer depends on how one historically locates camp. At the time, as I have argued in *Incongruous Entertainment*, when musicals flourished in the studio system and homosexual acts were illegal, camp was the social practice of gay men, supplying them with a rhetoric for responding to straight culture from the viewpoint of the closet. Camp was a kind of open secret, the means by which gay men identified themselves to other gay men while still passing as "straight." So it relied on certain codes—of dress, behavior, jokes, adjectives, tastes, favorite authors and stars—all manifesting what Joshua Glenn refers to as "engaged irony" with the various binaries that defined straight values (Glenn 1997: 15). Camp was thus a means of disrupting the seeming stable relation of form and content, surface and depth, low and high cultures, bad and good tastes, deviance and norms, margin and center. Whereas straight culture privileged the latter terms in those binaries, camp overturned the hierarchy to celebrate the former, more "debased" terms and the pleasures they identify. Camp reception can be generally understood, then, as a mode of reading and viewing that emphasizes forms, surfaces, low culture, bad taste, deviances, and margins. And as a coded means of openly engaging in covert communications, the camp style of Hollywood musicals could signal a kind of imagined exchange between queer filmmakers and queer viewers, at least in the minds of the latter.

Camp style, moreover, was also very much part of drag culture, not because gay men stereotypically identified with femininity but because camp treated with irony that straight way of thinking of homosexuality as the inversion of normative heterosexuality; from this perspective, camp recognized the performativity and incongruity of genders, detaching sexed demeanors from sexed bodies. Drag was not about a man passing as female but about his *performing* as one; hence gestures, posture, inflection, makeup, costume, hair, bosoms, all tended to be overstated in drag as opposed to, say, cross-dressing in order to pass successfully as the other gender or transvestitism as a source of erotic pleasure. One sign of the camp attractions of musicals was the frequency with which the genre's stars inspired drag acts and personae, indicating how the theatricality inherent in their musical performances signaled that gender was culturally constructed, not a natural essence. As Esther Newton's ethnographic research shows, however, whereas in gay culture the drag queen expressed the incongruity of straight gender roles through performance, the resident wit and clown in a social group was considered "the camp," the person whose engaged irony fully recognized and mocked that incongruity. Historically speaking, according to Newton's investigation, the subject matter of camp was incongruity, its style was theatrical, and humor was its strategy (Newton 1979: 106).

All of these factors account for how, as a style originating in and defining a queer sensibility standing apart from heteronormative tastes, camp celebrated excesses of all sorts. Whereas in the 1930s, 1940s, and 1950s camp was a guilty pleasure because sexual dissidence was legally a crime and camp was a common means of engaging with men as a queer and avoiding arrest, today camp is a guilty pleasure because it bypasses conventional standards of good taste and high art. As camp entered the mainstream in the 1960s, primarily through Susan Sontag's famous essay, "Notes on Camp," and Andy Warhol's paintings, collages, and graphics, it became affiliated with Pop Art. Subsequently, camp became detached from its original queer ground and is now used to describe ironic responses to "bad," over-the-top artifacts from the past as a means of reveling in their excesses with laughter from an ahistorical distance. Simply put, though, to appreciate something *as* camp, a response external to the object, is not the same as appreciating it for its camp.

With their over-the-top moments of spectacle, robust color schemes, female stars taking center stage, overt theatricalization of gender roles, musicals have always lent themselves to both types of camp reception. Indeed, reading through and around the romantic hetero-sexual narrative in a sense replicates how queer practitioners of camp themselves read dominant culture from the outside, overturning the inside/out binary and the privileges afforded to those inside culture as opposed to those left outside because of their sexuality. Many of the musicals were made in part by men and women with a perceivable queer sensibility, as evident at moments in a script's dialogue, in delivery of those lines, in the staging of numbers, and in the sets and costumes. Regardless of being unable to locate their camp intentionality with any degree of surety, queer audiences then and now could at least experience a sense of inferred camaraderie with the filmmakers as if the filmmakers were winking meaningfully to them through the film. By the same token, then and now, straight audiences could simply enjoy a musical as Pop Camp, enjoying its outlandishness and laughing not with it but at it.

Twentieth Century-Fox's *Gentlemen Prefer Blondes* (1953), based on a hit Broadway musical but heavily revised for the screen, exemplifies both a camp sensibility at work in its texture and a history of camp responses to that texture. Briefly, the musical recounts the exploits of two American showgirls who travel to Paris. Lorelei Lee (Marilyn Monroe), is a gold digger and proverbial dumb blonde whose eyes light up whenever she sees diamonds. Her best friend and colleague, Dorothy Shaw (Jane Russell), values love over money, repeatedly falling for poor men against Lorelei's advice. The plot concerns Lorelei's on again–off again–on again engagement to Gus Esmond (Tommy Noonan), a wimpy man controlled by his wealthy father, and Dorothy's attraction to Ernie Malone (Elliot Reid), a private eye hired by the elder Esmond to spy on Lorelei when she and Dorothy sail to France. Complications arise when Lorelei persuades Sir Frances "Piggy" Beekman (Charles Coburn) to give her his wife's diamond tiara and, though pursued to Paris by an insurance investigator, Lorelei refuses to return it. All ends happily, though, when the tiara is returned, Lorelei convinces the elder Esmond that she is not as dumb as she acts, and she and Dorothy have a double shipboard wedding to their respective suitors.

An important early essay by Lucie Arbuthnot and Gail Seneca stresses this film's feminist content. They do not explicitly read the musical as camp, though their argument lays the ground for taking their insights further and developing a camp reading. They distinguish the *pretext* (in the double sense of something coming "before" the text and serving as its excuse or cover story), which is the narrative I have just described, which concentrates on the romantic entanglements and endorses heterosexual coupling as a woman's goal, whether for money or love, from the *text*, which concentrates in numerous ways on the close friendship of the two women and which dominates the film throughout its ninety minutes. In the text they notice, for instance, how visually, in the two stars' "look, stance, use of space and activity," as well as their costumes, and camera shots and lighting, Dorothy and Lorelei resist the expected objectification of showgirls (Arbuthnot and Seneca 2002: 78). Although viewers may watch and enjoy the film solely for its pretext, the writers conclude, the pretext itself "scarcely threatens the text of female friendship. Even as they sing lyrics which suggest that heterosexual love is crucial for women, Monroe and Russell subvert the words through their more powerful actions" (84).

The pretext/text distinction is a useful one for it enables one better to appreciate a queer camp texture coexisting with the standard Hollywood romance plot of *Gentlemen Prefer Blondes*. That plot is simply a pretext for something else that the film puts into play. To start with, the emphasis on female friendship in *Blondes* questions its supposed male/female dual focus. Whereas the pretext encourages one to see a dual focus organized around Lorelei and Gus (she: beauty, flirtation, performing, and he: wealth, sincerity, reacting), a stronger dual focus emerges around Lorelei and Dorothy (blonde/brunette, marrying for money/marrying for love, innocence/worldliness, untruthful/candid, manipulative/direct, pragmatic/romantic), reconciled through their loyalty to each other. Alexander Doty thus reads *Blondes* as a bisexual text, which is to say he sees an erotic undercurrent to their friendship despite their overt heterosexual drives. Comparing this musical to director Howard Hawks's other nonmusical buddy films which, like *Only Angels Have Wings* (1939) and *Red River* (1948), trace the same kind of homosocial to heterosexual trajectory that Altman now ascribes to the musical genre, Doty notes how *Blondes* "keeps the narrative events representing the women's emotional commitment to each other running parallel to, and intertwined with, those representing their relationships with men" (Doty 2000: 133).

Doty looks very closely at the film to support his claims of how the strong emotional current to the women's friendship underscores every action and number in the film and can be called "erotic" in its affect due to its "queer charge" (132). His analysis is subtle and detailed, but what he notes about the ending is worth repeating here. The closing shots of the double wedding, which Arbuthnot and Seneca also discuss, occurs like this: a two-shot of Lorelei and Dorothy looking at their diamond rings; a two-shot of their grooms, Gus and Malone; a four-shot of the two couples as the wedding ceremony begins; a tracking shot that pushes the men to the margins and out of frame in order to focus on the two women smiling at each other in medium close-up, celebrating them as the central couple, as if Lorelei and Dorothy are marrying each other (Doty 2000:134).This is a very campy moment as the text ironically comments on its pretext by visually putting forward a queer couple in its closing moment; even though one may presume that neither woman is lesbian in the pretext, the text itself enables one to enjoy wholeheartedly this film's pleasures from the queer perspective for which Doty argues. The text, in other words, is "passing" as its straight pretext, which is also to say that the romance and gold-digging plots are simply the pretext for a film that knocks the musical genre's heterosexual bias on its head.

The musical numbers make the camp sensibility of *Gentlemen Prefer Blondes* even more pronounced. The most obvious example is Dorothy's rendition of "Anyone Here for Love?," a song not in the Broadway score by Jule Styne and Leo Robin, but written for the film by Hoagy Carmichael and Harold Adamson. Frustrated by the indifference of the twenty muscular members of the Olympic team also traveling on the ocean liner, a lascivious Dorothy complains of her plight in song to the female passengers also in the ship's gymnasium. Singing, she strides around and between the athletes, all flexing their muscles and wearing only brief flesh-colored shorts, who go through various gymnastic routines and pay no attention to her until the very end of the number when, diving over her into the ship's swimming pool, one man accidentally pushes her into the water.

This number, staged by Jack Cole (who was gay), is visually excessive in its display of male flesh and contextually excessive since it is driven by Dorothy's desire for all the men. "Doesn't anyone want to play?" she interjects at one point. "I like a beautiful hunk of man/ but I'm no physical culture fan," she sings. Russell herself wears a black halter top and full-length black trousers, and her delivery of the song, along with her expression and movement as the men ignore her to concentrate on their exercises, suggest at once (1) the frustration of a highly sexualized female cruising for anonymous sex since the men have no

Figure 3.7 Dorothy (Jane Russell) wonders if there is "Anyone Here for Love?" in *Gentlemen Prefers Blondes* (1953, Twentieth Century-Fox)

names and are interchangeable as bodies, (2) a mocking impersonation of femininity that exaggerates female aggression in an era where women were supposed to be passive and subordinated to men, and (3) a queer reflection on unbounded gay desiring (as if Dorothy were a drag queen). The number, in short, inverts the traditional desiring male gaze of classic motion pictures by configuring the choreography of the muscle men through Dorothy's gaze; it reverses the conventional objectification of showgirls in musicals by objectifying the men's nearly naked bodies; and it allows for a rather explicit gay male as well as a female gaze at the gymnasts.

Lorelei's solo number, "Diamonds Are a Girl's Best Friend," the signature number from the stage version, is camp in a different way. Performed as a show number, Lorelei ostensibly professes her own motto: a gentlemen's kiss may be fine, but she prefers diamonds. The number exaggerates the character's gold-digging mentality, indicating the performativity underlying it. "I can be smart when it's important," Lorelei, the supposedly dumb blonde, subsequently tells Gus's father. In its set design, choreography, and costuming "Diamonds" points out how her persona is just that, a mask she wears for men. Thus Lorelei— in a long pink strapless gown with a large bustle tied in a bow, her arms gloved, a thick sparkling choker on her neck, matching bracelets on each wrist and long dangling earrings—sings to an ensemble of men, all identically dressed in tuxedos and all holding up big red hearts, about who will get her attention, "men who give expensive jewels."

As she sings, Monroe's gestures further suggest an overexaggerated emphasis on her sexuality as a performance for the men. More scantily dressed showgirls, meanwhile, stand motionless as part of chandeliers or holding candelabras, adorning the deep red background of the set. They can be viewed as an objectification of women or, taking into account the outlandishness of that treatment, as a mocking of the kind of objectification Busby Berkeley made famous in his outlandish numbers, and even a jab at the female chandeliers in the "Stairway to Paradise" number of the lauded *An American in Paris* (1951). At another point a dozen ballerinas come out, their costumes matching Lorelei's in their color and bows, and she sings to them, claiming a camaraderie with women as she sings that the gender stakes of the sexual game are unequal because the men themselves are unavailable since they are married.

The "Diamonds" number can be watched as a camp performance of Monroe's exaggeration of a "soft" femininity in contrast with Russell's exaggeration of a "hard" femininity in the gymnast number. Lorelei's performance of femininity in her number as well as the plot is determined by the unequal states of courtship, for as she also tells Gus's father, "Don't you know that a man being rich is like a girl being pretty? You wouldn't marry a girl just because she's pretty, but my goodness, doesn't it help?" After "Diamonds" concludes, the French gendarmes arrive to arrest Lorelei for stealing Lady Beekman's tiara. But it has in turn been stolen (by Sir Frances) from Lorelei; so while

Figure 3.8 Lorelei (Marilyn Monroe) sings "Diamonds Are a Girl's Best Friend" in *Gentlemen Prefer Blondes* (1953, Twentieth Century-Fox)

she reunites with Gus and wheedles the cost of a replacement from him, Dorothy goes to the court disguised as Lorelei. Her disguise suggests how "Lorelei" is but a costume, a pose one wears; and when she reprises "Diamonds" in the courtroom, Dorothy's performance is more mannish in her delivery and mannerisms, contrasting with the softness of Lorelei's performance of the song, likewise suggesting a kind of female drag, one woman impersonating another. That Marilyn Monroe's performance of "Diamonds" lends itself to such a reading finds additional support in how it has been repurposed by popular culture as camp by Madonna's video of "Material Girl" (1985) and Nicole Kidman's "Sparkling Diamonds" number in *Moulin Rouge!* (2001).

5 HISTORICIZING THE MUSICAL THROUGH ITS INTERSECTIONALITY

An intersectional approach in the social sciences and humanities is:

> the study of intersecting social categories—such as race, gender, and social class—with which an individual identifies. Intersectionality uniquely addresses a holistic understanding of the lived experiences of an individual within a society. It is the recognition that social outcomes cannot be properly explained by investigating independent social categories and treating them as stand-alone variables.
>
> (Guittar and Guittar 2015: 657)

An intersectional approach to a film often requires one to read textual details symptomatically, looking for indirect references to historical currents, problematics, pluralities, and ideological tensions. An intersectional approach, moreover, has been particularly valuable for feminist analyses that link gendered identities to cross-sections of race, ethnicity, nationality, and class, but its utility applies to other issues as well such as place, as I shall show by looking at the opening sequence of a seemingly "frivolous" Hollywood musical.

The Gang's All Here (1943) is a Twentieth Century-Fox musical directed by Busby Berkeley and starring Alice Faye, Carmen Miranda, radio personality Phil Barker, and Benny Goodman and his orchestra. Subsequent chapters will return to Faye and Miranda's star imagery and to this musical itself as an exemplar of director Berkeley's visual signature. Right now I just want to examine its opening sequence.

The Gang's All Here begins with Aloysio de Oliveira singing "Brazil" in Portuguese. His face can be seen in the left corner of the frame, half of its shape cloaked in darkness, the other half illuminated. He moves closer to the camera until his face fills the center of the frame in a close-up, then the camera moves away from him as diagonal lines fill up the screen. The camera now discloses a ship in port, the S.S. *Brazil*, as an unseen chorus picks up the song. With the orchestra continuing to play its melody after the singing ceases, passengers disembark from the boat as crewmen unload its cargo: sugar, coffee, tropical fruit. As the fruit is lowered it stops above Carmen Miranda's head, which is adorned with a hat that looks like a bowl of fruit. She now sings "Brazil," backed by her band. Phil Barker arrives with a brass band to welcome her—and we discover we are not in Brazil after all but in New York. "Got any coffee on you?" he asks Miranda, to whom he presents the key to Broadway.

At this point the camera moves back to disclose the number's location on a nightclub stage as Miranda performs "You Discover You're in New York," the city where, for example, you are in a café that you may think is in Rio but you are really in the Big Apple, the melting pot of ethnic foods, entertainments, and people. She sings the entirety of the song, dancing in her platform heels and twirling her exotically costumed body. Then she dances off the stage to the nightclub floor. Anglo-looking showgirls, all dressed identically in black, pick up the song, each woman singing a lyric in sequence until they get to star Alice Faye, who winks at the spectator as she sings her line. The showgirls then go onto the nightclub stage, their bodies effaced by its darkness so that, rhyming with the opening, only their faces can be seen until they disappear entirely, leaving Miranda alone in the frame to finish

Figure 3.9 Carmen Miranda discovers she is in New York in *The Gang's All Here* (1943, Twentieth Century-Fox)

the song. Done singing, she turns to find Barker and gives him a bag of coffee. "Now I can retire," he opines.

To recap: although it initially appears to be set in Brazil, once "You Discover You're in New York" the scene is suddenly transformed into both the stage setting of the New Yorker nightclub and a fantasized, intersectional view of New York City that links the song's celebration of the locale's ethnic hybridity with the number's own projection of spatial, geographic, and cultural hybridity, evoking the popular impression of the city in the mid-1940s. New York at that time, travel writer Jan Morris recalls, was "a splendid fulfillment." "It was the Future about to occur." As she also puts it, "Seen in magazine photographs, in propaganda leaflets, or in the backgrounds of Hollywood musicals, Manhattan looked all panache, all rhythm, all good-natured dazzle, all Frank Sinatra and Betty Grable" (Morris 1987:7–8).

The vitality and excitement of 1940s New York City made visible some dramatic ideological realignments that were occurring in American culture at large and would be studied in depth beginning in the 1990s: what George Chauncey has analyzed in *Gay New York* (1994) was the reorientation of gender and sexual identity around a stricter hetero/homosexual binary; what Michael Denning has analyzed in *The Cultural Front* (1997) was the agitating presence and then effacement of a politicized labor force; and what Matthew Frye Jacobson has analyzed in *Whiteness of a Different Color* (1998) was the invention of a Caucasian identity. Put simply, all three historians argued that, during the period from the 1930s to the 1950s, cultural perceptions of sexuality, gender, class, ethnicity, and race were in the process of being contested and, ultimately, regulated more tightly as more monolithic, overlapping ideological categories; moreover, these scholars' research focused attention on New York City as a particular site for illustrating that cultural ferment. The city's paradoxical position in this history was very much bound up in its widespread association with energy, motion, and entertainment since that representation served to mask, while ultimately catching, the complexity and turbulence of its social heterogeneity with regard to the intersections of sexualities, genders, classes, ethnicities, and races—the hybridity that "You Discover You're in New York" celebrates through the intersections of its clashing images (Brazil/New York, Portuguese/English, tourists/entertainers, global foods/local eateries, Carmen Miranda/white showgirls).

The cultural significance of New York City, moreover, was represented by the well-circulated image of "The Great White Way": Times Square, the Broadway mainstem, and surrounding midtown thoroughfares. This area, where the big movie palaces, legitimate theatres, and other nightspots were located, received the greatest amount of national publicity since it was designed, beginning with the location of the two great train terminals (Penn and Grand Central stations), as a site for leisure and consumption. Before Prohibition the area was perceived as a carnivalesque convergence of the city's classes akin to an amusement park, a liminal district offering high and low entertainment to residents and tourists, one set off by the more notorious Hell's Kitchen to the west and the more regulated Fifth Avenue shopping district to the east, distinguished by the vibrant electric lighting that not only turned night into day but flooded the senses with advertisements, giving the area its nickname. By the late 1930s, commerce in the Times Square area had changed in its character if not its reputation, with, for instance, the high-priced cafes of the earlier era moving to the east, and night clubs like Billy Rose's wildly successful Diamond Horseshoe just off of Broadway taking their place; the new venues, designed as mass entertainment, were aimed at a middle-class audience, and they often recreated tame versions of the area's past in revues and stage shows.

Musicals of the 1940s like *Coney Island* (1943) that represent New York at the turn of the century or through the halcyon days of its already gone vaudeville era marked a comparable displacement of the entertainment district's present. This is one reason why the opening of *The Gang's All Here* with its celebration of present-day New York in its variety stands out so strikingly. Indeed, some scholars consider musicals to be evocations of carnival due to their camp appeal, not to mention their reliance on color, spectacle, dancing, and plots resulting in mistaken identities, sexual misadventures, and comic transgressions of the sort that characterize the narrative of *Gang's*.

In any event, intensified by the way that the war economy brought people from different US regions and of different class affiliations to the Times Square district for varying sorts of consumption and relaxation, by the 1940s the bourgeois tone of the area exemplified effacement of the ideological shifts that I have alluded to, but at the same time it made them more visible than elsewhere. For the Broadway–Times Square area of the 1940s was still a somewhat rowdy intersection of high and low, control and abandonment, with burlesque on one thoroughfare and legitimate theater on another, with double features, arcades, prostitution, and gay cruising on 42nd Street, young bobbysoxers lined up to watch Sinatra and a first-run movie at the Paramount on 43rd, and older, respectably dressed playgoers entering Sardis for dinner on 44th before going to see Rodgers and Hammerstein's *Oklahoma!* at the nearby St. James theatre.

"You Discover You're in New York" registers these intersecting currents because it treats the Times Square district as a metonymy of New York's cultural heterogeneity. Thus, for instance, when the number begins by segueing somewhat abruptly from "Brazil" to discovering you're in New York, it projects a carnival mood for the city through Miranda; yet with the unloading of that cargo, the number also recognizes the city's economic role in the realignment of US power over commodity production and trading in the Western hemisphere during the war. The number not only puts forward Times Square as the real port of entry into New York, it names the city itself "Broadway," in the process drawing a connection between the importation of one kind of commodity in one part of Manhattan island (sugar, coffee, fruit) and the circulation of another kind on The Great White Way (musical entertainments like this number with Carmen Miranda).

The song's lyrics thus celebrate how New York embraces all ethnic differences through their commodification as mass entertainment—"On Broadway, in Harlem, or Greenwich Village too / You'll see a lot of places that will seem like home to you." What the lyrics depict is how, rather like Miranda, whose thick accent and colorful costume instantly mark her ethnic and gendered appearance as "different" from the "proper" singing and "respectable" all-black outfits of the white showgirls, the city absorbs signs of Otherness into itself through show business, the homogenized whiteness of which the showgirls visualize until they disappear in the darkness much as Aloysio de Oliveira does in the number's opening. Although white bourgeois New Yorkers may have forgotten the intersections of sexuality, gender, class, ethnicity, and/or race in which they found their identities, this number in effect tries to jar their memory but does so playfully, joking about but not subverting the twinned ideologies of whiteness and capitalism that encourage this cultural amnesia. Thus after the number, Miranda and the showgirls bring patrons such as the wealthy suburbanites, Edward Everett Horton and Eugene Pallette, to the dance floor, teaching them the "Uncle Samba."

So while the song concludes, "In case you're missing the point/ You're in a typical joint / On gay Broadway," it states throughout how New York has the paradoxical ability to retain ethnic and other differences in the vast, if commercialized, display of its cultural heterogeneity, with the city showing off its abundant multiplicity by offering it up for consumption as food and drink, sex, and entertainment in a club very much like the one in which this number is set, the New Yorker. Thus the number's mobile camerawork, intricate staging, and intersections of Brazil and New York, of Portuguese and English, of Miranda's gyrating body and the staid showgirls, all serve to link its own spectacle with the cultural hybridity of the city itself through the mediation of a "Broadway" that is "gay" for being joyous and exuberant but also, as likely, for deviating from the norm while representing it.

CONCLUDING THOUGHTS

All five approaches to reading musicals discussed in this chapter do not ignore narrative but help to foreground the significance of numbers by showing how and what they can mean; and while I have looked at each approach separately with a single case study, there is no reason why two or more of them cannot be integrated in your readings or set in tension with each other (for instance, doing a camp reading of Top Hat due to its comic characters and mistaken identities alongside a dual focus reading, or doing a dual focus reading of Gentlemen Prefer Blondes by focusing on the male and female characters as inhabiting different spheres of empowerment alongside a camp reading).

And if narratives move a film linearly from beginning to end, these approaches look at musicals more laterally; they do not have to ignore the linear arrangement of numbers nor forget the narrative, but they do not let either be the ultimate factor in determining what and how a musical means. A lateral understanding of musicals in fact makes sense given how numbers invite repeated viewings. This is why numbers from old musicals now have an afterlife all their own on YouTube. One may complain that such excerpting does damage to musicals because it rips numbers from their narrative placement and function. But a lateral understanding of classical musicals makes sense in terms of how they were exhibited at the time of their release in continuous showings, which meant that audiences often entered in the middle of films, getting to the endings before they saw the beginnings. The roadshow musical changed all of that because their exhibition was designed to start with everyone already seated in the movie theatre, although subsequent runs of those films were continuous too. Today, of course, exhibition has changed and audiences are now habituated to seeing films from start to finish; nonetheless, numbers are frequently previewed online as part of a film's promotion; fans recreate them, repurpose them in mash-ups, or repost them as is on YouTube; and Blu-ray and DVDs encourage a lateral viewing of sorts through the pause, reverse, and chapter search buttons.

4

STARS OF THE CLASSIC MUSICAL

Because they have traditionally been designed as star vehicles tailored to the talents and personae of a studio's contracted actors, musicals have also been approached through and appreciated for their main players. It is customary, in fact, for fans to refer to characters by the stars' names, an indication of how transparent their performing appears on film and how their star images provide the basic ingredients of the roles they play. In many ways, stars working in musicals stretched themselves through their numbers more than their characters, especially since their screen personae usually determined their roles. Since limitations of space prevent me from covering major stars whose careers in musicals peaked by the late 1930s—Al Jolson, Eddie Cantor, Ruby Keeler, Dick Powell, Ginger Rogers, Eleanor Powell, and Jeanette MacDonald—I concentrate on those stars of the 1940s and early 1950, the genre's heyday during which studios churned out one musical after another and most were popular and profitable. The chapter concludes by looking at the two big names who came to prominence in the era of roadshow musicals during the 1960s.

Metro-Goldwyn-Mayer is the obvious place to start since this studio's motto was "more stars than there are in the heavens." And when talking about MGM's musicals the star that comes immediately to mind is **Judy Garland** (1922–1969), who worked at Metro from 1936 through 1950. Much has been written about Garland's personal troubles during her last years at MGM—her tardiness and absences, her addiction to pills—as well as the source—studio execs worried about her weight so they had doctors put her on amphetamines to control her weight and pep her up during the day and sedatives at night so she could sleep. Garland was a natural born talent who took direction quickly and did not need much rehearsal to nail down a number or a scene; when she performed for the camera she gave 110 percent of herself. Indeed, her difficult behavior during her last five years at MGM may have expressed resistance to the studio's control of her body and even a way not to perform when she knew she was not at her best.

Before her screen debut Garland was part of a vaudeville act with her sisters. She started at MGM as an adolescent and quickly made an impression due to her powerful voice, which was described as an adult's voice in the body of a child. Her break came in 1939 with lead roles in The Wizard of Oz and Babes in Arms, the latter musical opposite another child star who grew up at MGM, Mickey Rooney. Garland had already costarred as the girl next door in several of Rooney's Andy Hardy films. Though Oz gave Garland her signature song in "Over the Rainbow," Babes was the much bigger success at the time, leading to the cycle of "backyard musicals"—Strike Up the Band (1940), Babes on Broadway (1941), and Girl Crazy (1943) came after Babes in Arms—in which Garland and Rooney play teens who, for some good cause, get the neighborhood kids together to put on a big show. With For Me and My Gal (1942) and Presenting Lily Mars (1943) Garland proved that she could carry a film with her name alone above the title, and the huge grosses for Meet Me in St. Louis (1944) and The Harvey Girls (1946) confirmed her star status. Thereafter, as well as appearing in guest star sequences in MGM's all-star musicals, she received top billing over Gene Kelly in The Pirate (1948), Fred Astaire in Easter Parade (1948), and Van Johnson in In the Good Old Summertime (1949). However, when her behavior became more erratic and disruptive, with her tardiness or absences delaying production, she was fired from several high-profile projects. Her final MGM film was *Summer Stock* (1950) opposite Kelly.

Making a triumphant return to vaudeville at the Palace theater in New York in 1951, Garland's post-MGM career was primarily as a concert performer in arenas or nightclubs, with her Palace theatre engagement and her Carnegie Hall recital in 1961 the famous highpoints. The live two-disc recording of the latter won four Grammys and topped the *Billboard* charts for seventy-three weeks including thirteen weeks in the number one spot. Garland had already done records for Decca while at MGM and in the 1950s recorded several well-regarded albums for Capital. Her one outstanding film after leaving MGM was the musical remake of *A Star Is Born* (1954) at Warners, which gave her a second signature song, "The Man That Got Away." However, after big openings the film did not do as well as expected, given its long shoot and large budget, so the studio cut a half hour from the film, including two of Garland's numbers, and the reputation of the film subsequently suffered. Nominated for an Academy Award for her acting and expected to win, Garland lost to Grace Kelly. Garland did two dramatic pictures after her Carnegie Hall comeback and had a television variety show on CBS that lasted only a season. Her final picture, a musical filmed in London, was *I Could Go On Singing* (1963); its narrative has been viewed as self-reflexive commentary on her later career.

On screen Garland presents a mix of girlish innocence and ordinariness that is then deepened by the sophistication of her singing, in no small way due to Roger Edens' and Kay Thompson's arrangements and their mentorship. Typically, in her pictures she sings at least one slow, often plaintive ballad like "The Boy Next Door" in *Meet Me in St. Louis* and one up-tempo tune like "The Trolley Song" in that same film. The studio had doubts about her lack of conventional screen beauty, in contrast, say, with her costars in *Ziegfeld Girl* (1941), Lana Turner and Hedy Lamarr, so especially in her early musicals, Garland's characters often bemoaned her "in-betweenness," as one of her songs put it, or her physical difference from more typical Hollywood beauties. She was just under five feet, high-waisted with long legs, and was reportedly difficult to costume, so when watching a Garland film notice how her gowns tend to create the illusion of a longer torso. An androgynous or cross-dressing element was added to her image from the clown and hobo costumes in *The Pirate* ("Be a Clown") and *Easter Parade* ("A Couple of Swells"), respectively, the fedora and tuxedo jacket in *Summer Stock* ("Get Happy"), and the baggy shirt and black tights in *A Star Is Born* ("Someone at Last"). Androgyny became central to iconic imagery of Garland, too, especially the fedora and tuxedo jacket.

As an actress, Garland often inflected her dialogue with a knowing sense of camp humor, and she later brought that same camp wit to her concerts and television appearances when recounting stories about her days at MGM. Although always popular with women and girls, another central feature of Garland's iconic stature is her legendary gay following. Richard Dyer accounts for her appeal to gay men by attributing it to three factors. First, while representing ordinariness on screen, the

Figure 4.1 Judy Garland sings "Get Happy" in *Summer Stock* (1950, MGM)

intensity of Garland's singing, the energy and pep of her characters, and her off-screen post-MGM biography suggest an inability to conform to heteronormality that parallels the difficulty of remaining ordinary experienced by many gay men. Second, Garland's androgyny disrupts normative gender roles and notions of glamour, emphasizing their artifice and theatricality. Third, Garland's own camp attitudes, developed through her collaboration and close friendships with gay people like Edens and director Charles Walters at MGM, means she is not turned into a camp star by fans but offers them a source of identification through her camp-inflected performances. (See Dyer 2004: 137–191.)

JUDY GARLAND IN *THE HARVEY GIRLS* (1946)

In *The Harvey Girls* Judy Garland plays Susan Bradley, a spirited young Midwestern woman who travels west as the mail-order bride of a man she has never met in person although his letters have made her fall in love with him. Unbeknownst to her, saloon owner Ned Trent (John Hodiak) has written the letters for his friend, the prospective groom. Susan discovers the ruse as soon as she arrives in Sandrock so she joins the women she has met on the train to work as a Harvey Girl. According to the opening titles these women waiting tables at the Harvey chain of restaurants "conquered the west as surely as the Davy Crocketts and the Kit Carsons." Not surprisingly, Susan and her new friends help to domesticate the unruly male-dominated town, and she and Trent, who has been the target of her ire after she discovers his trickery in penning those letters, also predictably fall in love.

The musical builds upon Garland's star persona in multiple ways. It develops comedy out of her diminutive stature, contrasting her ordinariness with the statuesque showgirls who work at Trent's saloon, the Alhambra, and the rowdy men who patronize it. In particular, Garland's smaller size and plainer costumes stand out in contrast with the more statuesque figure and more boldly colorful and revealing gowns worn by Angela Lansbury, who plays Em, the Alhambra's headliner and a rival for Trent's affections. By the same token, Susan's spunk and assertiveness when confronting Em, the showgirls, Trent, and the other antagonists to the restaurant's "civilizing" presence, underline her difference from those Harvey Girls who leave immediately as soon as they are threatened with gunshots. *The Harvey Girls* pokes fun at Westerns and that genre's construction of masculinity since female characters demonstrate the grit, courage, and risk-taking of "Davy Crockets and Kit Carsons," as opposed to the men, who are timid (Ray Bolger's blacksmith character) or corrupt (Preston Foster's judge) or ambivalent, torn between his saloon's profits and the peaceful valley outside Sandrock (Trent).

Garland's performance shows she is in on the gender/genre parodying insofar as, like her line readings, her physical comedy enables a viewer to laugh *with* the actress and not *at* her character. In one scene, all the meat has disappeared from the Harvey House. Suspecting it has been stolen and is being stored at the Alhambra, Susan takes two guns from a customer's holster and goes there to retrieve the stolen goods. She peaks under the saloon doors, and enters, waving the guns wildly but in a way that indicates their weight and that she does not know how to shoot. Once having retrieved the steaks, she returns to Harvey House. Trent has ordered one rare steak and, making good on his order and believing he was responsible for the stolen meat, she delivers what he asked, literally, handing him an uncooked T-bone on a plate. In another scene, the Harvey Girls and the Alhambra's showgirls get into a fight, and though she is in it at the beginning and shown throwing her fists this way and that, Susan gets tangled up in a tablecloth and ends up sitting on the staircase, holding a statue of a semi-nude lady in her lap, looking mystified and blowing hair off her face.

Figure 4.2 Judy Garland in *The Harvey Girls* (1946, MGM)

Garland, of course, sings throughout the musical, which opens with her standing at the rear of the train performing her solo, "In the Valley (Where the Evenin' Sun Goes Down)." However, although this is a Judy Garland musical (she alone gets top billing), she shares the musical program with her costars. Angela Lansbury, albeit dubbed, has two show numbers. Virginia O'Brien sings "The Wild Wild West" as she shoes a horse after the new, inexperienced, and very citified blacksmith (Ray Bolger) has passed out. O'Brien, Garland, and Cyd Charisse (also dubbed) sing "It's a Great Big World" to build up their courage collectively. Kenny Baker sings and Charisse dances to "Wait and See." Bolger does a spirited dance solo. Garland and he dance to "Swing Your Partner Round and Round," which she sings but so do Marjorie Main and a chorus. Garland blends into the chorus as the Harvey Girls chant their motto, "The Train Must Be Fed."

Interestingly, "My Intuition," Garland's duet with John Hodiak, was filmed but cut from the release print, so her love interest and the romance plot are confined solely to plot. Trent and Susan do marry in the film's final moments (just as they organize the dual focus structure of *The Harvey Girls*), but his absence from numbers relieve the pressure on Susan/Garland to conform to expectations of heterosexual romance: what *The Harvey Girls*, lacks, in other words, is a straightforward love song for Garland as well as a duet with her lover. What Susan longs for in the first number, "In the Valley," is abstract and vague, localized in the landscape of the West and not directed to a person, even though she is traveling West at this time to meet the fiancé she has not yet met in the flesh. This song is more reminiscent of "Over the Rainbow" than of "The Boy Next Door."

Figure 4.3 Judy Garland sings "On the Atchison, Topeka, and the Santa Fe" in *The Harvey Girls* (1943, MGM)

The big production number in *The Harvey Girls* is the Oscar winning "On the Atchison, Topeka, and the Santa Fe," which is at once a fabulous Garland solo and a production number. It opens with the saloon's African American waiter (Ben Carter) singing the chorus, which gets picked up by and passed along to various townspeople, singly and in groups, until the town's entire population, it seems, sing it together as they await the train's arrival. The song then passes to the train's engineer and boilerman, to Marjorie Main and the conductor outside the rear car, and, as the train arrives, to Ray Bolger, Virginia O'Brien and the rest of the Harvey Girls, who sing it from windows as the train speeds by the camera. Once the train comes to a stop, cowboys sing their appreciation of the arriving women, who then recite their own introductions during the song's bridge. Finally, as the music becomes more melodic Garland leaves the train. In a single long take she sings the verse and a slower version of the chorus, as she moves around the number's expansive set, never missing her marks. She sings to members of the large ensemble as she comes upon them in small groups, touching them, wrapping arms, sitting down and swaying with them in sync. A cut to another take then has her moving with the rest as the conductor calls, "All aboard!" The tempo of the music quickens and everyone joins in. With Garland in front they line up alongside the train to sing in unison and wave, simulating the thrust of the engine revving, as the Atchison, Topeka, and Santa Fe speeds away. The number ends with the camera moving in for a closeup of the star.

If you cannot imagine musicals designed around a swimmer instead of a singer or dancer, someone at MGM could, and **Esther Williams** (1921–2013) was one of their biggest stars from the mid-1940s through the mid-1950s. Before MGM hired her, she was a championship swimmer whose plans to compete at the 1940 Olympics were curtailed by the outbreak of war in Europe which caused that event's cancellation. When she accepted MGM's offer, she insisted on a year of acting, singing, and dancing lessons before being cast in films. Her break came with the Red Skelton musical *Bathing Beauty* (1944), which featured elements in her swimming numbers and water ballets that became her trademarks: tight-fitting one piece bathing suits, diving that became increasingly dangerous, underwater photography, and synchronized swimming with an ensemble of young women, their movement in perfect sync with Williams's as if they were the Rockettes on stage at Radio City Music Hall. Williams costarred with the same actors frequently too: with Skelton in *Neptune's Daughter* (1949) and *Texas Carnival* (1951) as well as *Bathing Beauty*; with Van Johnson in *Thrill of a Romance* (1945), *Easy to Wed* (1946), *Duchess of Idaho* (1950), and *Easy to Love* (1953); with Ricardo Montalban in *Fiesta* (1947), *On an Island with You* (1948), and *Neptune's Daughter*; and with Howard Keel in *Pagan Love Song* (1950), *Texas Carnival*, and *Jupiter's Darling* (1955).

Because she was a passable singer who was sometimes dubbed, aside from the swimming sequences the musical numbers in Williams's films tended to be assigned to her costars or to specialty acts. But that is not to minimize the musical impact of her swimming sequences as numbers in their own right. They were carefully choreographed and scored, and increasingly featured her in daring stunt work that did not rely on a stunt double. Her swimming numbers were again received with awe by audiences when included in the compilation films *That's Entertainment* (1974) and *That's Entertainment II* (1976). And if Gene Kelly danced with the animated Jerry the Mouse in *Anchors Aweigh* (1945), Williams swam with Tom and Jerry in an animated dream sequence in *Dangerous When Wet* (1953).

Williams was a rather unusual musicals star because of her athleticism and muscularity, which did not detract from but did redefine her screen femininity. A natural performer who seemed not to be acting but was just being "herself" on screen, she often played a professional woman with a mind of her own. In *Neptune's Daughter*, for instance, her character goes from swimming competitively and winning awards to co-owning a company making women's swimsuits. She knows her way around every aspect of the factory, does all the designs for the suits, and professes not to have any interest in men or romance. (Of course she finds it eventually with Ricardo Montalban.) More to the point,

Figure 4.4 Esther Williams swims with Tom and Jerry in *Dangerous When Wet* (1953, MGM)

despite the romance plots of her films, Williams's athletic body was always front and center in her swimming numbers, challenging the era's conventions of a soft and compliant femininity. For even while showing off her figure, thereby seeming to conform her body to that of a showgirl, the one-piece swimsuit focused attention on her muscular arms, broad shoulders, and strong legs. Similarly, the swimming numbers in Williams's films showed off her feminine grace and eloquence in the water but they also made evident her risk-taking and daring stunt work, as when she worked with Busby Berkeley on *Million Dollar Mermaid* (1952) and *Easy to Love*.

MGM promoted the light-skinned, bourgeois bred, svelte, sophisticated **Lena Horne** (1917–2010) as the first African American movie star. While the studio did not cast her as maids, as was the practice when using black actresses who did not fit the Mammy stereotype, it failed to give Horne many character parts. Rather, she typically played "Miss Lena Horne, nightclub performer" in one or two specialty numbers in an otherwise all-white musical, enabling her appearances to be excised in many Southern markets. For that matter, in her debut for MGM, two unbilled musical appearances in *Panama Hattie* (1942), the visual treatment encouraged some viewers and journalists to mistake her for a Latina, an association reiterated in the setting and costuming for some subsequent numbers, such as "Brazilian Boogie" in *Broadway Rhythm* (1944) and "Love" in *Ziegfeld Follies* (1946), even though by then she was better known to screen audiences. What this hybridity may have tried to capture was

> Horne's position as a woman who could pass for white, vocally as well as visually, but who is nonetheless unproblematically incorporated into black entertainment and who self-consciously incorporates elements of black musical tradition into her performance without merely abandoning the white ones.
>
> (Dyer 2012: 121)

Scholars have followed Horne's own lead, as expressed in her one-woman Broadway show, *The Lady and Her Music* (1981–1982), by examining her cool and remote presence onscreen. As Kirsten Pullen observes about Horne:

> Her film performances, mediated by MGM's training and dictates and structured by the demands of naturalist acting, revealed Horne as a dignified and even aloof black woman. Her persona offered a sharp contrast to stereotypes that suggested primitivism, excessive sexuality, and comic overemotionalism.
>
> (Pullen 2014: 103)

Despite receiving star or costarring billing, Horne was almost always a narratively static figure; furthermore, in terms of how they were set, lit, shot, and arranged in space, her numbers usually looked different from the film containing them, enhancing her marginality and vestigial position for Hollywood. She may have been fashioned as the first mainstream black female star, but, except for her roles in the all-black musicals, *Cabin in the Sky* (1943) and *Stormy Weather* (1943), she was rarely given the opportunity to be a leading lady. MGM let her contract lapse in 1950 and while her film career was curtailed, she became a celebrated cabaret and nightclub performer.

Gene Kelly (1912–1996) came to Hollywood from Broadway, where he had started out as a dancer, landed the title role in Rodgers and Hart's landmark musical *Pal Joey* in 1940, and choreographed *Best Foot Forward*. Though producer David O. Selznick brought Kelly to Hollywood, because he did not make musicals Selznick sold Kelly's contract to MGM. There Kelly costarred with Judy Garland in *For Me and My Gal* (1942). However, his innovative use of screen dance was first revealed when loaned to Columbia Pictures for *Cover Girl* (1944), a Rita Hayworth vehicle that was an enormous success. Assisted by Stanley Donen, Kelly devised "The Alter Ego Dance," where his character moves in perfect sync with a ghost-like image of himself as he works out through the dance whether or not to let Hayworth leave his Brooklyn nightclub and accept an offer to star in a Broadway show. At MGM, and again with Donen's assistance, Kelly danced with Jerry the Mouse in a musical sequence in *Anchors Aweigh* (1945), another popular film that earned Kelly an Academy Award nomination for Best Actor. His film career was then interrupted by his service in World War II. Upon his return, he starred in *The Pirate* (1947) with Garland, and a broken ankle prevented their reunion in *Easter Parade* (1948). Reportedly, although Busby Berkeley was the credited director on Kelly's next musical, *Take Me Out to the Ball Game* (1949), Kelly and Donen unofficially directed it.

Kelly came into his own at Metro first with *On the Town* (1949), which he officially codirected with Donen and which was the first postwar musical to go on location, and then with the Academy Award–winning *An American in Paris* (1951), directed by Vincente Minnelli, who had also done *The Pirate*. Kelly costarred one last time with Garland in *Summer Stock* and worked again with Minnelli on *Brigadoon* (1954). Aside from *An*

Figure 4.5 Gene Kelly dances with his "alter ego" in *Cover Girl* (1944, Columbia)

American in Paris, Kelly is best known for the three films that he codirected musicals with Donen: *On the Town, Singin' in the Rain* (1952), and *It's Always Fair Weather* (1956). As collaborators, both men were involved in every aspect of each film, though generally speaking Donen devised the camera shots and angles while Kelly staged the dancing. During the filming of *Fair Weather* Kelly and Donen apparently fought, their collaborative friendship collapsed, and they never worked together again. Kelly's final musical at MGM was *Les Girls* (1957), directed by George Cukor. Thereafter, although he acted on film and television, and still danced in a few pictures, such as *What a Way to Go* (1964), *Les Demoiselles de Rochefort* (1967), and *Xanadu* (1980), Kelly concentrated on directing. His biggest movie project was *Hello, Dolly!* (1969).

Kelly's dancing stands out for his athleticism and muscularity, not to say his inventiveness and keen sense of performing for the camera's eye, but he also integrated his ballet training into his choreography. He tends to dance with male costars like Frank Sinatra in *Anchors Aweigh* and Donald O'Connor in *Singin' in the Rain* as often as with his leading ladies, yet is probably best known for his solos: the title number of *Singin' in the Rain*, the dance with his alter ego in *Cover Girl*, the newspaper dance in *Summer Stock* (1950), the dance on roller skates in *It's Always Fair Weather*. His musicals routinely give him the same kind of character, too: an all-American Joe bonded with his buddies, with whom he seems most comfortable; his initial pose as a somewhat arrogant and pushy womanizer, though, gets softened by his attraction to his leading lady, who brings out the more sincere, shy, and romantic fellow hidden by the outwardly aggressive behavior and his camaraderie with his buddies (for more on Kelly, see Cohan 2005: 149–199).

GENE KELLY IN *SINGIN' IN THE RAIN* (1952)

Singin' in the Rain looks back at the coming of talkies and end of the silent era, albeit with an affectionately satiric eye. It opens in 1927 at the gala premiere of *The Royal Rascal*, starring the famous team of Don Lockwood (Kelly) and Lina Lamont (Jean Hagen). Both stars are glamorously dressed and pretentious, though Don is smart and Lina is not. The joke is that her beauty belies her shrill, high-pitched voice, so the studio makes sure to let Don be the romantic team's spokesman. Fleeing over-jealous fans who rip his clothes for souvenirs on his way to the post-premiere party, Don saves himself by jumping into a passing car driven by Kathy Selden (Debbie Reynolds). When he puts the moves on her, thinking he can exploit his movie-star stature, she responds by critiquing his silent film acting as "nothing but a shadow on film, a shadow. You're not flesh and blood." Although she claims to be an aspiring actress in the theatre, it turns out that Kathy is a Coconut Grove dancer hired to jump out of a cake at the postpremiere party. When Don confronts her there, she throws a pie at him but hits Lina by mistake. Lina, angry and jealous, gets her fired from the Grove. After searching for her, weeks later Don finds Kathy working as a dancer at the studio, and they acknowledge their mutual attraction.

Figure 4.6 Kathy (Debbie Reynolds) tells Don (Gene Kelly) that he is "nothing but a shadow on film" in *Singin' in the Rain* (1952, MGM)

The success of *The Jazz Singer* (1927) convinces the studio to convert to sound, but Lockwood and Lamont's first talking picture, *The Dueling Cavalier*, has a disastrous sneak preview, threatening the stars' future. Don, Kathy, and best friend Cosmo Brown (Donald O'Connor), decide to take advantage of Don's background in vaudeville and save his career by turning *Dueling Cavalier* into a musical. But what to do about Lina? She is a triple threat, as Cosmo observes, since she cannot sing, dance, or act. He then gets the inspired idea of having Kathy dub Lina's singing and speaking. On the day before the premiere of the newly titled

Dancing Cavalier, however, Lina threatens the studio head with the power of her ironclad contract and he agrees to pull Kathy's credit as her voice double. The new musical is a smashing success; Lina finally gets to make a speech after the premiere screening, but since she cannot sing, Kathy is placed behind the curtain with Lina miming to Kathy's voicing of a song. Don, Cosmo, and the studio head pull up the curtain, exposing the fakery, Don announces that Kathy's is the voice the audience loved, and a new starring team in musicals is formed—Lockwood and Selden.

A much-studied moment occurs in *Singin' in the Rain* when, reunited with Kathy, Don wants to tell her how he feels but cannot: "I'm such a ham. I guess I'm not able to without the proper setting." He leads her onto an empty soundstage where, adjusting the lights, he sets the scene with a romantic mood, places her on a ladder, turns on a wind machine, and sings "You Were Meant for Me." This scene exemplifies the masculine persona of a Gene Kelly character. Outwardly, as when he and Kathy first meet or at the premiere of *The Royal Rascal*, he is aggressive, self-confident, boastful, sometimes even predatory with a woman who catches his eye. But it is all a pose, a mask covering up the more insecure, shy, and inarticulate man who needs a number to express himself honestly. Indeed, his description to Kathy of the scene he is imagining for her right before he begins to sing "You Were Meant for Me"—"a lady is standing in her balcony in a rose-trellised bower, flooded with moonlight"—recalls the moment in *Anchors Aweigh* when Kelly imagines the romantic, swashbuckling self wooing Kathryn Grayson, which belies the wolf in a sailor uniform that has been his outward demeanor.

The Comden and Green script of *Singin' in the Rain* deepens one's sense of the Kelly persona by linking his dualism to its larger themes, which raises questions about the authenticity of stardom, the illusionism of cinema, and the uncertain dialectic of sound and image that the talkies bring about. Don's account to the radio audience of his rise to stardom at the premiere of The Royal Rascal makes this apparent. On the one hand, he offers an account that presents himself as the product of an elite upbringing by parents who introduced him to classics of the theater, gave him "rigorous training" at the Conservatory of Fine Arts and an "exclusive" dramatic academy, after which he and Cosmo toured "the finest" symphonic halls before arriving in Los Angeles where he was flooded with offers from the movie studios. On the other hand, what we see on screen differs considerably from what Don narrates. As boys he and Cosmo tap dance in pool halls, they sneak into a nickelodeon, they perform on amateur night, in burlesque, and in vaudeville where they do "Fit as a Fiddle."The audience there boos the duo but Don states, "Audiences everywhere adored us."When he gets to LA, though, Don slips up, his language momentarily connecting his speech to what we see: he says, "we were stranded—we were staying here …" This montage, in sum, equates sound (Don's narration to the crowd outside Grauman's Chinese theatre and the radio audience) with fabrication, and the image (what the film shows us onscreen) with truthfulness. Indeed, the non-diegetic audience experiences this clash when the diegetic audience boos a number we might want to cheer. "Fit as a Fiddle" is a fabulous and funny piece of footwork by Kelly and O'Connor, the first of many smash numbers in Singin' in the Rain.

What exemplifies the disastrous preview of Dueling Cavalier is also a tense relation of sound and image. For in addition to Lina's ineptitude when recording her voice, Don's jettisoning of the scripted dialogue so that he can inanely repeat "I love you" many times over, and the inconsistent volume of ambient noise, during the preview the image and disc go out of sync, so that when Lina opens her mouth the villain's voice speaks and vice versa. The subsequent decision to dub Lina makes an even greater problem of sound because it suggests that movie stardom, like the voice, can be falsified. Extrafilmically, Kelly and codirector Stanley Donen raise this problem to an even higher degree by having Jean Hagen, who plays Lina, dub Debbie Reynold's speaking voice when Kathy is dubbing speech for Lina. This is a conundrum indeed, especially since talkies made possible the arrival of musicals that Singin' in the Rain is celebrating. Like Don's own stardom, which is hammy in his silent historical melodramas but authentic in musicals, sound must therefore be redeemed before the final credits.

Kelly's dancing supplies the means of healing the breach between sound and image that causes much of the film's big comedy sequences, just as it is the means by which Don reveals his true self to Kathy, belying the glamourous but false movie star posture he exhibits in the opening. Dancing, especially when we see the full bodies of the dancers, cannot be faked as easily, for dancing is the embodiment of the performer. It addresses Kathy's critique of silent film acting: the dancer is not a shadow on film but gives the illusion of being flesh and blood, of being embodied. Thus Debbie Reynolds's singing voice was not dubbed in her numbers where she also dances.

Most of the great dancing numbers, moreover, occurs spontaneously and are detached from the satire of the silent era: in addition to dancing with Kathy to "You Were Meant for Me," Don does a frenetic and fabulous tap duet with Cosmo in "Moses Supposes"; the two men and Kathy tap to "Good Mornin'," and Don goes it alone in the rain to the title song. The "Broadway Melody" ballet, which is ostensibly from the new modern portion of "Dancing Cavalier," recasts Don's origin story from the opening as dance: the ballet recounts the story of Don's hoofer arriving in New York and moving from burlesque to vaudeville to the Ziegfeld Follies. Furthermore, Kelly's two encounters with a mute Cyd Charisse, the moll who attracts but leaves the hoofer for a gangster, occurs simply as pure dance, drawing on the stars' training in ballet (and her muteness in this big number addresses the problematic of talking women, Lina's whose voice threatens Don's career and Kathy's whose voice criticizes it). The "Broadway Melody" ballet, in sum, revises Don's opening montage by embodying sound, the refrain the hoofer sings, "Gotta dance," in his dancing body.

Figure 4.7 Gene Kelly has "gotta dance" in the Broadway ballet sequence of Singin' in the Rain (1952, MGM)

To be sure, the tapping sounds in the dance numbers was dubbed after the fact and not always by the person doing the dancing, just as the music and singing were prerecorded. Dancing covers over this rupture (which one can only hear, not see) due to the power of the image's illusionism, which has called into question the authenticity of sound from the beginning of Singin' in the Rain. Thus when Don and Kathy team for their "Singin' in the Rain" film in the closing moments, sound has been safely and artfully subordinated to the image much as, in the diegesis, Don has been teamed with a more authentic musical costar suitable for the talkies.

Frank Sinatra (1915–1998) was the idol of teenage "bobbysoxers" during the World War II years. Known as "The Voice," he was the equal of the later Elvis Presley or Michael Jackson in terms of his popularity with teenagers, his embodiment of an untraditional male sexuality, and his lasting influence on music. Initially signed by RKO, where he made several low-budget musicals, Sinatra moved to MGM on loan for *Anchors Aweigh* (1945) and then, when RKO let his contract lapse, stayed at MGM on a five year-year contract. *Anchors Aweigh* cemented his persona during his tenure at Metro: he plays the shy, timid, virginal milquetoast opposite the more virile and assertive Gene Kelly, roles the two stars repeat in *Take Me Out to the Ball Game* (1949) and *On the Town* (1949). Sinatra plays this same wimpy type in *It Happened in Brooklyn* (1947) and *The Kissing Bandit* (1948).

In all these musicals Sinatra sings romantic ballads, exploiting his famous voice, yet the films call attention to his unmanly physical appearance and behavior, and in most of them he does not get the woman he first has eyes for. He loses Kathryn Grayson to Kelly in *Anchors Aweigh*, Grayson to Peter Lawford in *It Happened in Brooklyn*, and Esther Williams to Kelly in *Take Me Out to the Ballgame*. In the latter musical and *On the Town* the more aggressive Betty Garret pursues and woos a reluctant and virginal Sinatra. As Karen McNally concludes, "Sinatra's incoherent screen image at the studio stems from the extent to which his characterizations draw on aspects of his image as a singer while attempting to neutralize its problematic core of intentional sexualization and self-objectification" (McNally 2010: 96–97).

MGM dropped Sinatra when his popularity waned in 1950, yet he famously made a comeback, winning an Oscar for a supporting role in *From Here to Eternity* (1953). Thereafter his screen persona altered but, though he continued to record albums and to perform in nightclubs and became better known for his dramas and comedies, he still made musicals: *Young at Heart* (1954), *Guys and Dolls* (1955), *High Society* (1956), *Pal Joey* (1957), *Can-Can* (1960), and *Robin and the Seven Hoods* (1964). In the title role that Gene Kelly had played on Broadway, Sinatra's Pal Joey well typifies his post-MGM persona. With his fedora tilted over his forehead and a trench coat swung over his shoulder, Joey is a swinger, a lady-killer, a man about town, a night owl, and this persona became attached to off-screen perceptions of Sinatra too, especially during his Rat Pack days in Las Vegas and Reno/Lake Tahoe, memorably reflected in *Oceans 11* (1960).

Significantly, while Sinatra's voice continued to define him on records, in cameo appearances, on television specials, in nightclubs and concert halls, musicals still remained a crucial element of Sinatra's persona for the duration of his career. If he did not sing theme songs written by his friend Sammy Cahn (even when not starring in the film), then Sinatra did covers of them on his albums. More strikingly, in the middle of *Come Blow Your Horn* (1963), a romantic comedy, Alan (Sinatra) abruptly breaks into the title song, a call to arms to his younger brother Buddy (Tony Bill); a montage shows him singing in stores and on the street while supervising Buddy's make-over into a Sinatra-like bachelor. This sequence is a bona fide musical number in a comedy that is not a musical; yet the number does not disturb the texture of *Come Blow Your Horn* but seems perfectly consistent with it, because of Sinatra's history of starring in musicals. The number breaks the comedy's illusionism but nonetheless the moment seems believable as an aspect of Sinatra's screen persona and fame as one of the century's great singers.

Not counting his first screen appearance in MGM's *Dancing Lady* (1933), where he partnered with Joan Crawford in a production number, **Fred Astaire** (1899–1987) starred in ten musicals at Metro, but he also worked for most of the other companies as well. He first saw success on the New York and London stages when teamed with his sister Adele. After several hit shows she retired and he went solo in *The Gay Divorce* in 1932. RKO signed him, trying him out with

Ginger Rogers in *Flying Down to Rio* (1933), and then paired the couple in the film version of his stage hit, retitled *The Gay Divorcee* (1934). From that point on this popular dance team dominated film musicals during the 1930s in films such as the previously discussed *Top Hat* (1935) and are still affectionately called "Fred and Ginger." Astaire and Rogers made nine films for RKO during the 1930s and were later reunited for a tenth at MGM in *The Barkleys of Broadway* (1949).

Astaire freelanced after leaving RKO, doing *Broadway Melody of 1940* with Eleanor Powell, *Yolanda and the Thief* (1945) and *Ziegfeld Follies* (1946, though mostly filmed two years earlier) for MGM; *You'll Never Get Rich* (1941) and *You Were Never Lovelier* (1942), both with Rita Hayworth, for Columbia; and *Holiday Inn* (1942) and *Blue Skies* (1946), both with Bing Crosby, for Paramount, to list the highpoints of this period. *Blue Skies* was supposed to be his swan song in films, but he came out of retirement two years later to replace Gene Kelly in *Easter Parade* (1948). He was busy for the next decade, working at MGM on films such as *Royal Wedding* (1950), *The Band Wagon* (1953), and *Silk Stockings* (1957), the last two musicals opposite Cyd Charisse; returning to Paramount for *Let's Dance* (1950) opposite Betty Hutton and *Funny Face* (1957) opposite Audrey Hepburn; and moving to Twentieth Century-Fox for *Daddy Long Legs* (1955) opposite Leslie Caron. When traditional musicals faded in popularity in the late 1950s and the studios let their personnel go, Astaire did three award-winning television shows with Barrie Chase. He continued to act in several nonmusicals during the 1960s and 1970s. His last film musical was as the crusty father who steals the leprechauns' pot of gold in *Finian's Rainbow* (1968).

Throughout his career Astaire was an influential figure, whether with respect to his dancing on stage, in films where he innovated protocols for filming and editing dance that persisted for many decades, or in his television work. We also should not forget his influence on popular music; praised for the precision and eloquence of his phrasing, which songwriters and critics felt equaled that of his dancing, Astaire introduced in his films many songs that have become standards. Additionally, as Todd

Decker has discussed at length, Astaire was important in bringing jazz to the screen; he surrounded himself with leading musicians, arrangers, and composers regardless of their race and the music in his films was scored as complexly as the dancing it was mated to (see Decker 2011).

Astaire's screen persona likewise reflects the same qualities that made him so influential. He typically plays a performer, which creates logical reasons for his dancing to start with, has a debonair, sophisticated look (symbolized by his top hat and tails) yet rarely plays someone from the elite class, and is as crisp and eloquent in his speech and movement as when he sings or dances. As he got older and his female costars younger, he plays the role of a mature romantic mentor, a Pygmalion who teaches his youthful paramour about love and romance through his dancing. Nevertheless, even then, as in his earlier films with Ginger Rogers and Rita Hayworth, Astaire's dancing tends to even the gender playing field, so to speak, as later evident when partnering with the younger Cyd Charisse in their two films together or Vera-Ellen in *Three Little Words* (1950) and *The Belle of New York* (1952). Throughout his career, and even when the narrative purpose of a number was seduction and enchantment, for Astaire dancing with a woman was about both their bodies moving equally in space.

At Paramount the leading star of musicals was **Bing Crosby** (1902–1977), who came to pictures after establishing himself as a popular singer on records and radio. That success occurred as innovations in the microphone enabled Crosby to develop a clearly phased singing style that sounded deeper, more mellow, more intimate, yet more naturally masculine than the crooners who preceded him (see McCracken 2015). At Paramount his breakout film was *The Big Broadcast* (1932) after which he made on average three or four musicals a year until the early 1950s when he slowed down a bit. Among his many films, Crosby costarred with two major stage performers whose film careers never took off the way they did on Broadway—Ethel Merman in *We're Not Dressing* (1934) and *Anything Goes* (1936), and Mary Martin in *Rhythm on the River* (1940) and *Birth of the Blues* (1941). He is best known for his long-standing professional friendship with comedian Bob Hope, the other big star at Paramount who dabbled in musicals on occasion. Crosby costarred with Hope and Dorothy Lamour in the hit "Road" series of musical adventures in colonized countries: *Road to Singapore* (1940), *Road to Zanzibar* (1941), *Road to Morocco* (1942), *Road to Utopia* (1946), *Road to Rio* (1947), *Road to Bali* (1952), and *Road to Hong Kong* (1962). Additionally, Crosby and Hope appeared together on radio and Crosby made frequented cameo appearances, often in a sight gag, in Hope's comedies.

Crosby's success is fascinating because he was not like other stars of the genre. His musicals relied for the most part on his singing alone—his was one of the great voices of the twentieth century but, as Allison McCracken points out, "his persona offered a white masculinity that was extreme in its evacuation of emotion or desire" (McCracken 2015: 299). He typically does not look at his female lead when singing to her or she overhears him (300); and his dominant characteristic as an actor is his lack of affect: a Crosby character tends to exist on an even emotional plane despite crises that may be occurring around him. He thus represents a paternal form of stability and security, often in contrast with costars like Astaire in their two films together, *Holiday Inn* (1942) and *Blue Skies* (1946), or with Hope in their many "Road" pictures.

Crosby's characters, moreover, tend to represent a conservative view of patriarchy, personifying country life and small-town values more than urban living and modernity; this persona contrasts with later revelations about his abusive behavior to his four sons during his first marriage, his history of drinking and his first wife's alcoholism, and his coldness with coworkers on the set. For instance, in his Academy Award winning performance in *Going My Way* (1944), Crosby plays a priest, Father Chuck O'Malley, whom the Bishop sends to St. Dominick's church to solve its financial troubles (it owes on a mortgage and the bank wants to foreclose on the property). Father O'Malley is said to be "modern" which does not translate into progressive ideas but reflects tropes associated with Crosby's stable, paternal, masculine persona, which was reiterated in fan magazine accounts of his off-screen life: Father O'Malley sings, plays golf, turns a bunch of rowdy boys into an obedient choir, and saves the church by selling a song he has written.

Crosby repeated this character in *The Bells of St. Mary's* (1945) and also plays a priest in *Say One for Me* (1959). In *High Society* (1956), the musical version of *The Philadelphia Story* (1940), Crosby takes on Cary Grant's role; but whereas Grant is the epitome of fast talking, wit, and sophistication, playing the same character Crosby is more contemplative, casual, distanced, and slower in his delivery. When starring opposite Hope, whom he typically calls "Junior," Crosby plays the mature, more experienced and wiser partner to Hope's effeminate clown, who is frequently the butt of physical jokes and victim of Crosby's con-artist schemes (see Cohan 1999 and 2017b).

Crosby's film career lasted for thirty years, during which he recorded numerous hit songs and albums, including several Oscar winners, and regularly appeared first on radio with his own series and then in television specials and guest-shots. He also was a highly successful producer and business man, owner of several early television stations; one of the first stars to pre-record and edit his radio shows (most others' shows at the time were aired live), he invested in and his company helped to develop audiotape and videotape recording. Today Crosby is probably more remembered for his music than his acting (or his business acumen), so it is worth observing again that during his career he was one of the most popular movie stars working. From 1944 through 1948 he won the *Photoplay* award as Most Popular Male Star, and he is one of the few stars of musicals to have won an Oscar for his acting. Aside from his films with Hope and *Going My Way*, he is best known for *White Christmas* (1954). He first sang that iconic title song in *Holiday Inn* and sang it again in *Blue Skies*.

The biggest star in musicals at Twentieth Century-Fox was **Betty Grable** (1916–1973), the most famous pin-up of World War II whose signature feature was her legs, which for a publicity stunt the studio insured with Lloyds of London for a million dollars. The iconic pin-up featured her standing in a one-piece bathing suit, her exposed back to the camera, her face peeking over her shoulder.

Grable started in films by lying about her age, working in bit parts until the truth was discovered and she was let go for being underage.

Going to Broadway, in 1939 she eventually found success in a supporting role in *DuBarry Was a Lady* and Fox signed her. When Alice Faye had to drop out of *Down Argentine Way* (1940), Fox put Grable in her place and the popular musical made her a star. Fox then cast her with Faye and John Payne in *Tin Pan Alley* (1940). Grable appeared frequently with the same male costars, and she usually carried the musical burden. She was reunited with Don Ameche, her costar in *Down Argentine Way*, for *Moon Over Miami* (1941) and with Payne for *Footlight Serenade* (1942), *Springtime in the Rockies* (1942), which also featured her future husband, Harry James, and *The Dolly Sisters* (1945). She starred opposite Victor Mature in *Song of the Islands* (1942) and *Wabash Avenue* (1950), opposite Dick Haymes in *Diamond Horseshoe* (1945) and *The Shocking Miss Pilgrim* (1947) and opposite Dan Dailey, perhaps the costar best known for teaming with Grable, in *Mother Wore Tights* (1947), *When My Baby Smiles at Me* (1948), *My Blue Heaven* (1950), and *Call Me Mister* (1951).

Grable starred in several pictures a year and almost all were big earners for Fox, their profits often subsidizing the studio's more prestige fare. The musicals had thin plots, bouncy tunes, a bold yet lavish Technicolor palette, and Grable's perky, unassuming screen personality, peaches-and-cream complexion and blond hair, clear voice, and energetic dancing. Moreover, many plots were set at the turn of the century to give her persona a nostalgic sheen. Grable was considered the ideal (and very blonde and white) girl next door during the 1940s, which further accounts for the widespread appeal among GIs of her omnipresent pinup. Capitalizing on that photo, Fox starred her in *Pin Up Girl* (1944).

BETTY GRABLE IN *MOTHER WORE TIGHTS* (1947)

The opening of *Mother Wore Tights* typifies the trajectory of many Betty Grable show musicals, which often trace her character's transition from dancing wildly in saloons or vaudeville to the more refined and glamourous legitimate stage. As an off-screen chorus sings "M-O-T-H-E-R" ("M is for the million things she gave me," etc.), we see Grable, made up to look middle-aged, sitting on her porch in a wicker chair, knitting. The camera moves in, as a female voice says, "This is mother. Isn't she sweet?" Immediately, the film cuts to a younger Grable in a shiny black corset, with a cat's face on her breasts, another one on her head-band, and thick white fur trim accenting her hips; dancing, she does high kicks and waves her arms in circles, with a big smile on her face, all to the tune of "Ta-ra-ra-boom-der-ay." "Good heavens!" the voiceover continues, "Who'd dreamed she'd ever behave like this?" Grable turns, flips up the thick fur tail attached to her bottom, and, glancing back to the audience, raises a leg in a reverse knee bend and dances off stage. The voiceover belongs to Mother's younger daughter, Mikey, who narrates the musical, which recounts Mother's rise from bump-and-grinding in vaudeville to more refined dancing in revues.

Mother is Myrtle McKinley, who, starting out in the chorus of his act, partners with and marries Frank Burt (Dan Dailey). The couple go on the road together; when they have children, Myrtle retires until tempted by Frank to return to the stage. The narrative conflict arises when the older daughter, Iris (Mona Freeman), who has been consorting with wealthy friends while at boarding school, becomes ashamed of her parents' profession. She believes that "people on the stage don't have refinement." Well, in *Mother Wore Tights* they do, and they don't.

To ease her embarrassment, Myrtle and Frank invite Iris's classmates to a performance of their show in which they per-form "There's Nothing Like a Song" and several reprises of earlier numbers. The classmates love it but Iris runs out in tears, whether with relief or shame, it is hard to know—until the next scene, which has the third rendition of the film's theme song, "You Do." Frank first sings and dances to "You Do" in a fast and syncopated arrangement; he is dressed in a loud checkered suit with a straw hat, matching pink vest and oversized bow tie, and an artificial daisy pinned to his lapel. Accompanied by a bevy of chorus girls (including Myrtle), he treats it as a broad comic number that showcases Dan Dailey's nimble footwork. Later in the film, after Myrtle rejoins Frank on the road, on an elegantly adorned stage she sings a slow version of "You Do." Wearing a glamorous, floor-length, bejeweled gown, her hair piled high in ringlets on her head, and a diamond choker, she holds a large ostrich feather fan and is accompanied by four men in tuxedos. Importantly, this is not the Mother we saw at the film's opening for not only is Myrtle glamorously dressed but she rarely moves in the number, standing still or walking slowly while singing, one hand on hip, the other holding the fan. Finally, at the school graduation in the conclusion Iris reprises the song, backed up by her classmates, to show how much she loves her parents. The three versions of "You Do," in short, mark a progressive refinement of music, musical tastes, and Mother.

Figure 4.8 Betty Grable sings "You Do" in *Mother Wore Tights* (1947, Twentieth Century-Fox)

Like most Betty Grable musicals, the simple plot holds together an assortment of numbers that feature her singing and dancing, and Dailey was her first male costar who could really dance with her. Their half-dozen show numbers chart Myrtle and Burt's act from vaudeville to theatrical revues, reiterating the truism of the genre that "You Do" traces: yes, theater folk can clean themselves up well but they are neither as stuffy nor as snobbish as the elite class of wealthy people. Thus, at a Berkshires resort, where all the older wealthy guests seem half-dead, Myrtle and Fred bring life to the place and eventually get everyone to join in a singalong and even to dance.

As in her other musicals, too, Grable is somewhat fetishized as an icon of whiteness in *Mother Wore Tights*. The period setting allows her to wear her blond hair in piles of curls and waves on the top of back of her head; at times the extensions or wigs look like crowns or headpieces. In her show numbers she is typically costumed in white clothes that accent her blondness and pale skin. For instance, in the montage of "This Is My Favorite City," one of those vaudeville numbers that substitute in the lyrics the name of the town where the performers are playing, Grable wears different dresses, but each one is white.

But that fetishization should not detract from Grable's talent or the musical merits of *Mother Wore Tights*. While known for her dancing, she is also a decent singer with clean phrasing and warm tones. One number that highlights her talent is Myrtle's imitation of Frank doing "Burlington Bertie from Bow" in male drag, which makes him see elements in his own performance that he was not aware of and which prompts him to suggest that Myrtle and he team up. Lowering her voice, Grable parodies Dailey's performance of the number, and the parody makes good use of her timing, finesse with props, and facial expressions. As for their dancing, Grable and Dailey do not tap but perform a variety of often quick soft shoe moves. The spirited choreography takes full advantage of how well the two stars complement each other as musical performers.

The other major female star at Fox was **Alice Faye** (1915–1998). Faye was one of Fox Films' few assets when the bankrupt company merged with Darryl F. Zanuck's Twentieth Century Pictures to become Twentieth Century-Fox in 1935. The 1930s saw Fox finding Faye's persona; she played motherly types in Shirley Temple vehicles, *Poor Little Rich Girl* (1936) and *Stowaway* (1936) and wisecracking Jean Harlow types in musicals such as *365 Nights in Hollywood* (1934), *Music Is Magic* (1935), and *On the Avenue* (1935).

Two of Faye's best films from this period, which crystallized her stardom and persona, were *In Old Chicago* (1938) and *Alexander's Ragtime Band* (1938), both with Tyrone Power and Don Ameche. The latter musical established the formula of many Fox show musicals: the narratives recount a wide swathe of time and while the characters mature as the story progresses the actors never age a day. Faye starred again with Powers in *Rose of Washington Square* (1939), modeled on the biography of Fanny Brice, and with Ameche in *Hollywood Cavalcade* (1939), *Lillian Russell* (1940), and *That Night in Rio* (1941). Her signature song was the Academy Award–winning "You'll Never Know" from *Hello Frisco, Hello* (1943). Subsequently, until she departed Fox in 1945 and retired after a row with Zanuck, Faye was, like Grable, box-office gold for the studio. And as Fox did with Grable, the studio paired her repeatedly with the same leading men, Ameche or John Payne. She eventually returned to Fox and to the musical in 1962 for the remake of *State Fair*.

Faye is known best for her husky singing voice, contemplative approach to a song, and no-nonsense Hell's Kitchen-type personality and accent. In *Week-End in Havana* (1941), for example, she plays Nan Spencer, a shop girl at Macy's who has used her savings to go on a cruise that has been canceled in Havana due to the ship captain's misbehavior. Because she alone knows the real reason for the cancellation, the company sends Jay Williams (Payne) to get her to sign a waiver so they can settle with the other customers; she holds out, though, for her vacation, so Jay begrudgingly puts her up in an expensive hotel suite. Nan then directs almost everything that happens in the narrative, with Jay a hapless and passive bystander—until he falls in love with her. As she tells him, "I've never seen anyone work so hard at having a good time. ... You don't seem to know how to enjoy yourself." By contrast, Nan knows how to enjoy herself, is determined to do so, and will be the means of teaching enjoyment to Jay. Resorting to Hollywood cliché, she breaks the reading glasses he has worn throughout—and they kiss.

Furthermore, although Carmen Miranda has the big, spectacular numbers, Faye has the ballads. It takes a while for her to sing, too, which is to say that only slowly does Nan become absorbed into the musical "magic" of Havana. Miranda has three numbers in succession before Faye sings her first song, "Tropical Magic." The sequence begins with a male trio singing it in Spanish as Nan leaves Jay in the nightclub, watches sadly at the couples moving about, and wanders by herself to the terrace outside. Leaning against a pillar and shown in closeup, as Faye sings the English lyrics, her head and shoulders are still (in contrast with Miranda's whirling, swirling, twirling body in her numbers) and the motion of her eyes—she looks up to the dark moonlit sky, she glances around her, she looks straight ahead, she looks up again—suggest the thoughts and feelings motivating the song. Faye and Payne later reprise this song when, after their car crashes, they are brought back to Havana on a wagon; lying in the back on bales of hay, they sing it facing each other in medium closeup—and Faye's husky voice is deeper and fuller of emotion than Payne's brittle tenor.

Faye co-starred with **Carmen Miranda** (1909–1959) in *That Night in Rio* (1941), *Week-End in Havana* (1941), and *The Gang's All Here* (1943), and Grable appeared with Miranda in *Down Argentine Way* (1940) and *Springtime in the Rockies* (1942). Although she had star billing with her blonde costars and was one of the highest paid women in the movies, Miranda never played the lead but served as comedic support. Yet she always had several numbers that were outlandish and spectacular showstoppers. In *Week-End in Havana*, for instance, Miranda has four numbers in contrast to Fay's two songs plus that reprise.

Miranda was born in Portugal but her family moved to Brazil shortly after her birth. A successful entertainer there in nightclubs and films, she made a splash at the 1939 World's Fair in New York City and while performing at the fair also starred in a revue on Broadway for the Shuberts. Fox signed her and her first Hollywood appearance was in *Down Argentine Way*. Her numbers were shot in New York while she was appearing onstage there and inserted into the narrative as night club segments. Moving to Los Angeles, for the next several years Miranda starred in many of Fox's biggest hits; her characters were incorporated into the plots and her colorful costumes and wild production numbers were highlights. As her popularity cooled after World War II and her Fox contract ended, she moved to MGM where she costarred in *A Date with Judy* (1948) and *Nancy Goes to Rio* (1950).

From films like *Down Argentine Way, That Night in Rio, Week-End in Havana, Springtime in the Rockies*, and *The Gang's All Here*, Miranda became an icon of popular culture and inspiration for drag artists; she was imitated on film by celebrities like Bugs Bunny, Mickey Rooney, and Bob Hope, not to mention by scores of soldiers in various army shows during World War II. She was a self-knowing camp figure before camp hit the main-stream in the 1960s. With her over-the-top, luridly colorful outlandish costumes—which typically exposed her midriff, legs, and sometimes her hips, a turban often adorned with bunches of fruit, jingle-jangly bracelets, necklaces, and earrings, and tall platform shoes that enabled her to dominate the film frame—she was a "larger-than-life" presence (Pullen 2014: 139). Her presence was further accented by the constant movement of her hands, eyes, and hips as she danced. Miranda often performed in her native Portuguese and spoke fractured English in her dialogue scenes. She wore the same types of outfits in her scenes as well as her numbers, indicating the fluidity of her comic persona and her musical one.

To be sure, Miranda's characters were variations of an exotic yet comic Latin stereotype with names like "Dorita," "Rosita," and "Conchita." However, in personifying otherness in contrast with her blonde female costar (Grable, Faye), Miranda has been read as a disruptive female: her character interrupts the flow of the romantic narrative; she physically exudes female sexuality, however managed as comedy;

her exaggerated look, easily imported to drag acts, celebrates femininity as a masquerade; and although light-skinned herself, with elements of her costume retaining their origins in working-class and black Bahian culture, she heightens her racial and ethnic difference in comparison with the whiteness of her costars.

As Kirsten Pullen puts it, "Where Miranda nearly explodes, the white women are safely contained," positioned through the musicals' romance plots (Pullen 2014: 31). Hence Fox made Miranda a bona fide star of its musicals yet marginalized her from her films' romance plots except as a comic foil; even so, her excessive presence dominated her films whenever she was onscreen. For instance, just consider the opening of *Week-End in Havana*. It begins with a dissolve from a travel display to Miranda singing the title song. Her costume is outrageous but typical for her: the turban is adorned to look like the an exotic sea urchin; the red-and-white striped ruffled cloth of the turban matches the ruffled sleeves of her midriff; her skirt, with mesh exposing both hips, is a riot of magenta, white fringe, turquoise, more white fringe, more magenta, and two more layers of white fringe; on her neck are several necklaces composed of white and yellow shells that match her bracelets. Miranda does not really dance while singing so much as she remains a figure in perpetual motion: her eyes roll, her grin widens, her hips do not stop undulating, her arms do not cease moving up and down or across her stomach, as she sings. When she dances later in the number, she moves her feet in time with her arms and hips, her full skirt flowing in waves across the dance floor. Miranda's number here is an image impossible to forget, especially since this is the first of three of her numbers in succession and, whether performing in the nightclub or off-stage fighting with her lover-manager Caesar Romero or trying to seduce John Payne, her costuming is comparable throughout *Week-End in Havana*.

Columbia made a few A-pictures each year, many of them musicals starring **Rita Hayworth** (1918–1987). Hayworth is now remembered mostly for her film noir roles as the femme fatale in *Gilda* (1946) and *The Lady from Shanghai* (1947), for her famous pin-up pose that was the second-most popular during the war after Betty Grable's, and for being the epitome of Hollywood glamour in the 1940s. A Brooklyn-born Latina (Marguerita Carmen Cansino) whom her studio Americanized by molding her look (raising her hair line, coloring her hair red, changing her name, giving her diction lessons) yet never hiding her heritage, Hayworth was at the time also well known for her consummate dancing in musicals. Some consider her a better partner for Astaire than Ginger Rogers, as evident in *You'll Never Get Rich* (1941) and *You Were Never Lovelier* (1942). And while *Cover Girl* (1944) is now recalled as the musical that established Gene Kelly as a star and showed his inventiveness as a choreographer for the screen, it was extremely popular and a big money-maker for Columbia because of Hayworth. She subsequently confirmed her star wattage in *Tonight and Every Night* (1945) and *Down to Earth* (1947), neither of which paired her with a male star of commensurate dancing ability. Even when not acting in a musical, as in *Gilda*, Hayworth usually had several numbers that showcased her abilities as a dancer, yet not as a singer since Columbia almost always used a voice double—Nan Wynn, Anita Ellis, or Martha Mears.

Hayworth's star image was somewhat paradoxical, as Adrienne McLean has well explained. In press coverage and studio promotion, "Rita Hayworth's distinguishing and most publicized features become her Latin heritage, her ability as a dancer, and the fact that her good looks are the result of much manipulation" (McLean 2005: 39). Hayworth's glamour was shown to be authentic because it had been manufactured and the studio never papered over her Latinness but incorporated into its promotion her physical transformation from Hispanic Margerita Cansino to all-American Rita Hayworth. As a result, as Priscilla Peña Ovalle notes when discussing Hayworth's teaming with Fred Astaire, "her racial mobility, employing the codes of whiteness and non-whiteness," produced a star image with a new kind of sexuality, for she was "both desired and desiring" (Peña Ovalle 2011: 85). Finally, Hayworth's dancing displays a self-confidence and assertiveness as well as talent and training that gives expression to "her own felt subjectivity" despite how her films' narratives may ultimately work to contain her character (McLean 2005: 123).

RITA HAYWORTH IN *COVER GIRL* (1944)

Cover Girl perfectly registers Hayworth's persona—and the contradictions her star image attempted to manage. For in this musical, she is manipulated by the male characters yet ambitious in breaking out of the chorus; furthermore, while her character, Rusty Parker, is prized for her beauty, and turned into a glamourous figure, Hayworth's dancing invests Rusty with a sense of energy, movement, and agency that belies the machinations of the narrative which confine her to a romantic union either with working-class, Brooklynite, nightclub owner Danny McGuire (Gene Kelly) or wealthy, Manhattanite, theatrical producer Noel Wheaton (Lee Bowman).

Rusty is a dancer at Danny's club, and a member of the chorus in the first two numbers, "The Show Must Go On" and "Who's Complaining?" Both numbers feature the chorines, including Rusty, mainly as eye candy. She quickly leaves the chorus line, however: Rusty dances in the street with Danny and Genius (Phil Silvers) in "Make Way for Tomorrow," she becomes Danny's partner in another show number, "Put Me to the Test," and the couple make up after a quarrel offstage by dancing to "Long Ago and Far Away." In these three numbers Hayworth establishes Rusty as the dancing equal of Kelly. However, Rusty is also torn—satisfied to remain at Danny's club with him but desirous of a quick start to a bigger career. The chance to get ahead arrives with a modeling contest: *Vanity* magazine is searching for an unknown woman to feature her as the "Golden Wedding Cover Girl." Indeed, when Rusty quarreled with Danny it was about success—if one needs to pay one's dues and work one's way up slowly or if one could bet on a lucky break and find instant stardom.

Figure 4.9 Rusty (Rita Hayworth) and Danny (Gene Kelly) dance to "Put Me to the Test" in *Cover Girl* (1944, Columbia)

The publisher of *Vanity*, John Coudair, chooses Rusty because she reminds him of his long-lost love, Maribelle Hicks (also Hayworth in flashback), who turns out to be Rusty's late grandmother. Hayworth' two numbers in flashback as Maribelle, "Sure Thing" and "Poor John," allow her to be seen in period costume and they are framed doubly through the perspectives of young (Jess Barker) and older (Otto Kruger) Coudair. More important, as Coudair directs Rusty's makeover and transformation into a cover girl, and when he tells Danny that "beauty like hers demands certain things," which he can offer but the younger man cannot, the magazine publisher is projecting his fantasy about Maribelle onto Rusty. As Coudair admits, because of her close resemblance to Maribelle she makes the years disappear, which is also to say that managing Rusty's career and private life makes him forget that her grandmother humiliated him onstage with "Poor John" (the phrase his mother used when he brought

Maribelle home) and that Maribelle fled their wedding to marry the poor piano player whom she really loved.

Furthermore, Coudair encourages theatre producer Wheaton to pursue Rusty. Wheaton entices her into accepting the starring role in his new revue but also manipulates her into doing so. Not only does Wheaton enable Coudair to live out his fantasy of controlling Maribelle by separating her from her lover, but the younger man also projects his own desires onto Rusty. When he first sees her dancing at Danny's club, Wheaton is pushy and arrogant, and he never changes his attitude in his dealings with her; she may be an object of fascination to him, but she is still an object. To both men Rusty is Beauty Personified, not a real woman.

As noted already, *Cover Girl* is known for Kelly's innovative "Alter Ego Dance," in which he dances with a projection of himself to work out his conflicted feelings about Rusty's success—and what he thinks is her betrayal, since she has stood him up for their regular Friday night date. In fact, however, Coudair and Wheaton have tricked her into in a private meeting with the latter, who takes her to his empty theater to make his pitch. "The Alter Ego Dance" allows Danny to decide to let Rusty go, so although she has decided to stay at his club, he picks another fight with her, forcing her hand. She quits and becomes Wheaton's star and his fiancée, but her unhappiness is signaled by her frequent drinking. What this number and Wheaton's trickery may make one forget, however, is that, thinking she owes Coudair her presence at a party celebrating the anniversary of his magazine (the excuse Coudair gives her to get her to go off with Wheaton), she defiantly refused to stay to perform in the club's late show, despite Danny's order that she do so. The difference between Danny on one hand and Coudair and Wheaton on the other is one of class. For while Danny keeps insisting Rusty has freedom of choice, that he can say to himself during "The Alter Ego Dance," "If you really care about Rusty you'll let her go," means that he also thinks of her as a possession.

Hayworth's dancing in *Cover Girl* resists this objectifying view of Rusty, however. After all, whereas a cover girl is a still image, a dancer *moves*, her body expressing her subjectivity and engaging the viewer's gaze on her terms despite how men like Coudair may objectify her as a screen on which to play out their own fantasies. When he takes Rusty to his empty theatre, Wheaton asks, "Did you ever dance on a stage as big as this one? It's more like flying than dancing. The freedom of it." He tells her to close her eyes and whirls her around, but, as she dances alone to a reprise of "Make Way for Tomorrow," Rusty drops her fur stole and glides around the stage, twirling, arms stretched out, humming the tune, her long red hair flying as she spins. With her eyes closed and a smile on her face, she is dancing for herself, not for or to Wheaton.

Figure 4.10 Rusty (Rita Hayworth) dances for herself on the empty stage in *Cover Girl* (1944, Columbia)

The freedom Rusty/Hayworth exhibits is even more noticeable in the number representing Wheaton's show, "Cover Girl (That Girl on the Cover)." Its opening sequence displays numerous real-life cover girls, the models posing before an image of their magazine cover. The second sequence, however, shows that Rusty is "no stationary cover girl," as Jeanine Basinger remarks, but a dancer. The models are frozen images, meant to be looked at, whereas in the number proper Rusty seems to descend from the heavens, "a living, breathing talent. She is also free and unleashed, in control of her dance, the center of the universe" (Basinger 1993: 147). Waving her long arms as if she were flying, Rusty descends from the clouds and dances down a winding ramp, at the end of which a dozen identically dressed chorus boys greet her. While they sing the song's lyrics and line up to take her photo, as Rusty dances with two of them she is a moving target, remaining "fancy free" as the lyrics proclaim. She never stops moving during the entire number. At its conclusion, she ascends back to the heavens, alone.

Hayworth exhibits the same sense of exhilaration when dancing with Kelly in "Put Me to the Test," a tap number in which he at times pursues her, following her lead, but mostly they parallel each other's frantic footwork (and this kind of dancing with a female partner is not typical of Kelly's subsequent choreography at MGM). As in her solo dancing, here too Hayworth's graceful movement, extending her body with her long arms, gives the impression that for her to dance is to soar.

Hayworth's dancing helps one to look beyond the narrative confinement of Rusty by the various male characters. Basinger notices the plot's contradictions: despite the inevitable recoupling of Rusty and Danny, which gives an impression of negating the cover girl trajectory to stardom, she does become a star almost immediately after her cover girl appearance; what is more, she has genuine talent, warranting her departure from the chorus and Danny's club. In other words, she reaches stardom without Danny's help. On his part, Danny projects his ego onto Rusty just as Wheaton and Cordair do; he keeps telling her to live her own life but he passive aggressively wants her to stay in his show. He needs to dance with his alter ego, literally, to decide to let her go.

Thus while the narrative of *Cover Girl* insists that Rusty cannot be happy without Danny, "what it really shows is how Hayworth becomes powerful in and of herself after she is glamourized," put on the cover of *Vanity* and then given a show of her own (Basinger 1993: 147). Put another way, the narrative sends the message that love of Danny is more important than Rusty's stage success, that working hard is better than being rich, but only when the plot is cleaved from the numerous dancing numbers. For those numbers tell a different story about Rusty's cover-girl success, not to say about the liberation she expresses while dancing. Furthermore, when Rusty leaves Wheaton at the alter and returns to Danny, does that also mean she will give up her new career? After all, she is still starring in Wheaton's show while Danny closed his club as soon as he left and now has a job entertaining the troops. Rusty is the bigger star, which the closure on the couple's reunion wants us to forget.

An eccentric and often volatile comedian, **Danny Kaye** (1911–1987) came to film musicals after his breakout success in nightclubs and in a supporting role in Broadway's *Lady in the Dark* in 1941, in which he performed the kind of nonsensical tongue-twisting song that became his signature style. Beginning with *Up in Arms* (1944), he starred in a yearly film for producer Samuel Goldwyn and distributor RKO: *Wonder Man* (1945), *The Kid from Brooklyn* (1946), *The Secret Life of Walter Mitty* (1947), and *A Song Is Born* (1948). Thereafter he moved around, making *The Inspector General* (1949) for Warners, *On the Riviera* (1951) for Twentieth Century-Fox, *Hans Christian Andersen* (1952) for Goldwyn and RKO, until he signed with Paramount, for whom he made several pictures, most notably *White Christmas* (1954) and *The Court Jester* (1955).

Except for *Hans Christian Andersen* and *White Christmas*, Kaye's musicals are not traditionally structured. His numbers, almost always written by his spouse, Sylvia Fine, tend to be cleaved from the narratives as show numbers, patter monologues, scat improvisations, or fantasies. They give occasions for Kaye to display his vocal dexterity, physical agility, and inventiveness. His characters tend to be neurotic, timid, and shy around women, so the plots typically engage him in some sort of mistaken identity, disguise, or doubling in order to turn him into a more conventionally masculine version of himself: he is a timid librarian possessed by his dead identical twin brother, a show biz type, in *Wonder Man*; he is a milkman mistaken for a prizefighter in *The Kid from Brooklyn*; he is an itinerant performer mistaken for a government official in *The Inspector General*; he has a double whose identity he assumes in both *On the Riviera* and *On the Double*; and so on.

This repeated trope of his musicals suggests how a split personality is central to the Danny Kaye screen persona The various doubling plots contrast an inner but more real effeminate version of Kaye's character with the outer pretense of a more virile one, while often giving that more "manly" Kaye musical or comic routines calling his virility into question. The doubling thus raised the implication of a queer nonconformity that became attached to his persona despite the narrative's assertions of his characters' normative heterosexuality (see Cohan 2017a). At the same time, because of his carnivalesque wildness and nonsensical songs, Kaye was enormously popular with children, which became the definitive note of his later career. For instance, in 1976 he starred as Captain Hook/Mr. Darling and Geppetto/Boris Stroganoff in brand new musical versions of *Peter Pan* and *Pinocchio*, respectively, opposite women (Mia Farrow, Sandy Duncan) playing boys—and come to think of it, Kaye was playing doubled characters here, too.

The only actress other than Shirley Temple to top exhibitor polls for several years in succession, **Doris Day** (1922–2019) is best (and to my mind wrongly) remembered as the perennial virgin due to her very popular sex comedies with Rock Hudson, so one forgets her different persona in her first decade as a film star. Unable to get Judy Garland or Betty Hutton for *Romance on the High Seas* (1948), Warners signed Day, who at the time was a popular singer with the Les Brown Band as well as on radio. Though fourth-billed, Day was the lead character and the musical gave her a hit song with "It's Magic."

During her seven years at the studio her musicals ranged from show musicals to biopics to nostalgic evocations of turn-of-the-century Americana. With Gordon MacRae and Gene Nelson, she appeared in *Tea for Two* (1950); with those two and James Cagney in *The West Point Story* (1950); with Nelson in *Lullaby of Broadway* (1950); and with MacRae in *On Moonlight Bay* (1951) and *By the Light of the Silvery Moon* (1953), both based loosely on Booth Tarkington's "Penrod" stories. If not playing a young widow, as in *My Dream is Yours* (1949), she was tomboyish, adept at baseball and fixing cars, as in *Moonlight* and *Silvery Moon*. In *April in Paris* (1952) her chorus-girl character is rough around the edges, outspoken, scrappy, and disruptive, but also the figure who causes things to happen. In *Calamity Jane* (1953), Day plays a rough-edged, cross-dressing, masculine woman who guards the Deadwood Stage, is a sharp-shooter, is mistaken for a man when she travels to Chicago, and has no use for feminine adornments. Although she does get somewhat feminized and marries Wild Bill Hickock (Howard Keel), the man she has traded barbs with throughout the film, she stills wants to take her gun with her on her honeymoon. Despite their different plots and settings, *April in Paris* and *Calamity Jane* not only typify the nonconforming female Day tended to play in her musicals, but they also take advantage of her dancing skills as well as her singing.

Although Day did some nonmusical work while at Warners, she did not renew her contract and freelanced for the rest of her career. Her first role upon leaving Warners was as singer Ruth Etting opposite Cagney in MGM's musical biopic, *Love Me or Leave Me* (1955); the biopic follows the repercussions of Etting's decision to hook up with a gangster (Cagney) to further her career. She returned to Warners in 1957 for *The Pajama Game*, in which she plays a union organizer who puts her activism over

Figure 4.11 Doris Day as *Calamity Jane* (1953, Warner Bros.)

her romance with John Raitt. Day's final musical was MGM's *Billy Rose's Jumbo* (1962); however, it was seen as an old-fashioned, big budget throwback to the studio's salad days and was not a success.

For the most part Day is now better known for the romantic comedies she made after 1955, in which she balanced playing sophisticated career girls and mothers. Her nonmusical films still have her singing a title song and sometimes one additional number. Day's signature song, "Que Sera Sera," is from Alfred Hitchcock's thriller, *The Man Who Knew Too Much* (1956). There Day plays a former singer whose son is kidnapped, and the tune, which she sings with the boy early in the film, is the means by which her husband (James Stewart) rescues their child when she performs it at the foreign embassy where he is being held. Enriched by her warm, smoky voice, "Que Sera Sera" typifies the appeal of Day's nurturing, maternal and not virginal femininity, the other side of which is her tomboyish pluck and refusal to kowtow to male authority figures simply because she is female.

Although she had been a big success in New York and London in *My Fair Lady* from 1956 to 1959, had starred in Rodgers and Hammerstein's *Cinderella* on television to a massive viewing audience in 1957, and had returned to Broadway in *Camelot* in 1960, Jack Warner decided **Julie Andrews** (1935–present) was not well-known enough for the film version of *My Fair Lady* (1965) so he cast Audrey Hepburn instead. Walt Disney signed Andrews for *Mary Poppins* (1965), which won her an Oscar and made her a star. The megahit *Sound of Music* (1966) then cemented Andrews's fame and persona as the quintessential perky governess.

Andrews quickly moved on to dramas and romantic comedies but returned to musicals, each intending to expand her persona—*Thoroughly Modern Millie* (1967), *Star!* (1968), *Darling Lili* (1970), and *Victor/Victoria* (1982). However, she was never able to escape the "practically perfect" image of Mary Poppins completely. After the soaring heights of the 1960s her career leveled off, as she mostly worked with her husband Blake Edwards. His *S.O.B.* (1981) knowingly satirizes Andrews's screen persona, knocking down the sunny-sweet demeanor. In the queer friendly *Victor/Victoria* she plays a woman pretending to be as a man pretending to be a woman. Edwards later developed this film into a full-fledged Broadway musical. During the run, Andrews developed throat problems and botched surgery ended up ruining her singing voice. Nonetheless, she continues to act in films, to direct some regional stage productions, and to write children's books.

Many consider *Star!* to have been the tipping point of Andrews's career as a major, bankable star, its failure leading to the backlash against the sunny and sweet persona she had been identified with since *Mary Poppins* and *The Sound of Music*. There are many reasons for the box-office failure of and critical disinterest in *Star!* In addition to the changes occurring in the film industry and in the audiences for theatrical films, *Star!* could never have been the successful follow-up to *The Sound of Music* that Twentieth Century-Fox had imagined by bringing back that film's star and director, Robert Wise, in another roadshow musical. A biopic about the British and New York theater star, Gertrude Lawrence, just did not have the wide appeal of a Rodgers and Hammerstein musical aimed at a family audience. Most Americans knew little about Lawrence, who had been a famous theater actress in plays and musicals but made few films. To compensate for how she had been forgotten, the promotion and the script keep repeating that Gertie Lawrence was a star, as if simply insisting upon it would make it resonate with audiences; but sheer insistence does not make it so. Indeed, the decision to conclude the film after the opening of *Lady in the Dark* in 1941 (presumably to avoid dealing with her death and to end instead with her second marriage) meant that *Star!* does not include the one musical for which Lawrence might have been remembered, her final show, Rodgers and Hammerstein's *The King and I*.

More to the point, *Star!* characterizes Lawrence as the direct opposite of what moviegoers at the time loved about Andrews. In the film Gertie is quick-tempered, ambitious, and a scene-stealer; she is overly self-dramatic in her private life; she is extravagant, spending way beyond her means, and runs around with a fast set; in New York she has affairs with two men while her lover is in England (and it is not clear if she is being kept by him); and she is not maternal, resulting in her daughter's alienation. But this characterization also shows Andrews's own aim of dramatically stretching herself beyond the governess persona.

Still, *Star!* has its fans and has become a cult favorite, mainly because of the numbers. Andrews has fifteen, count 'em, *fifteen* numbers in *Star!* All performed as show numbers, well-staged by Michael Kidd, using songs by the likes of Noel Coward, the Gershwins, Cole Porter among others, with colorful costumes and sets, some with backup singers and dancers, they offer an anthology of Andrews' considerable talents and skill in selling many different types of songs. *Star!* is, in effect, two films in one: a straight biopic with a lumpy, episodic narrative about a theatrically compelling but unengaging actress and a smash musical revue starring Andrews at her best.

Barbra Streisand (1942–present) was already a singing phenomenon with best-selling albums, a career in cabarets and nightclubs, award winning television specials, and a 1964 stage hit as Fanny Brice in *Funny Girl* when she repeated that role in the 1968 film version, winning the

Academy Award for acting. Before *Funny Girl* premiered, she had already been signed for the film versions of *Hello, Dolly!* (1969) and *On a Clear Day You Can See Forever* (1970). Going to Hollywood under a six-picture deal with *Funny Girl* producer Ray Stark, Streisand did romantic comedies and dramas for him, most notably *The Way We Were* (1973). Her final picture for Stark was the musical *Funny Lady* (1975), a sequel to *Funny Girl*.

Streisand returned to musicals under her own shingle, producing another version of *A Star Is Born* (1976), for which she shared an Oscar with Paul Williams for their song "Evergreen," and directing herself in *Yentl* (1983). Though known for her musical roles because of her singing expertise, Streisand has acted in more nonmusicals over her career, and while she continues to perform in films on occasion she has never ceased to record albums, releasing over fifty. Aside from her numerous awards for singing, she has had an album hit the top of the Billboard charts each decade since the 1960s.

Streisand is perhaps the first star since Cantor and Jolson not to downplay her Jewishness but to incorporate it into her screen persona, starting with *Funny Girl*. Even when not explicitly playing Jewish, as in *Hello, Dolly!* (Dolly married the late Mr. Levi but was born Gallagher), she reads *as* Jewish due to her accent and inflections, not to say her energy and ambitiousness, and her character takes charge of the plot. A known perfectionist, all elements of a Streisand musical tend to focus on her even when appearing alongside established leading men like Walter Matthau in *Dolly*, Yves Montand in *On a Clear Day*, or Kris Kristofferson in *A Star Is Born*.

Funny Girl, for instance, uses only half of the Broadway score, incorporating in the place of the dropped numbers songs identified with Brice ("I'd Rather Be Blue," "Second-Hand Rose," "My Man"). In other words, with the exception of "If a Girl Isn't Pretty," the film jettisoned numbers performed by other characters in the stage version. Streisand has one duet with Omar Shariff ("You Are Woman, I am Man"), who sings briefly and tentatively; the remaining numbers record her self-confidence, self-assertiveness, and ambition from the get-go ("I'm the Greatest Star").

Due to the inconsistent fortunes of the musical genre since the 1960s, not to say how the genre has morphed into various subgenres that may or may not always be legible as musicals, no stars have been as firmly identified with musicals since Andrews and Streisand. Significantly, too, their musicals tended to be one-woman shows, some of them enjoyable and now memorable if only as opportunities to watch them perform.

As for the stars of musicals in the present day? John Travolta, Hugh Jackman, Zac Efron, and Channing Tatum all have the talent and have made occasional forays into the genre, but they have resisted becoming exclusively identified with musicals. Jackman, for instance, has done *Les Miserables* (2012) and *The Greatest Showman* (2017) but most of his appearances in the genre has been on stage; in films he is better known as Wolverine. Efron, coming off of *Hairspray* (2007) and the *High School Musical* trilogy (2006, 2007, 2008), turned down the remake of *Footloose* (2011) after first being attached to it because he did not want to become so firmly associated with musicals, although he did finally return to the genre as the second lead of *The Greatest Showman*. Female stars such as Meryl Streep, Anna Kendrick, and Emily Blunt have considerable singing talent, have starred in several successful musicals, but their filmography is also generically varied. Beyoncé Knowles and Christina Aguilera made *Dreamgirls* (2006) and *Burlesque* (2010), respectively, but neither film led to a crossover movie career, as musicals had done for singers Doris Day and Barbra Streisand in earlier eras.

Along with the absence of a home studio designing vehicles for its cohort of stars under exclusive contract, this state of affairs has as much to do with the industrial conditions of contemporary stardom as it does with the fact that fewer musicals are being produced yearly now. Today's actors, along with the talent agencies managing careers and often putting together production packages for them, seek a degree of generic diversity that the older studios seldom allowed for their stars. Thus none of today's stars come to mind for their almost exclusive association with the musical as was the case for the performers discussed in this chapter.

5

FIVE AUTEUR DIRECTORS

With a few exceptions, the musical genre is not director-driven. "There are no auteurs in musical movies. The name of the game is collaboration," Gene Kelly stated when accepting his AFI Achievement Award in 1985. An excellent account of the many hands that produced a musical can be found in Donald Knox's *The Magic Factory* (1973), the oral history of the making of Kelly and Vincente Minnelli's *An American in Paris* (1951). Although the book is now out of print, if you can locate a used copy or if your library has it, it is well worth your time for its documentation of the multiple contributions that comprised the finished look of this musical—and by extension, of any musical during the studio era—in its planning and execution.

One reason for the lack of much attention solely to directors (as opposed to the stars) by film scholars of the musical may be because the very collaborative nature of the musical mitigates a single author study focused solely on musicals. Furthermore, with the exception of Busby Berkeley, most directors of the genre worked in other genres, too—even Kelly himself did when wearing the director's hat. Some directors, moreover, such as Howard Hawks when making

Gentlemen Prefer Blondes (1953), concentrated on the narrative scenes and left the planning and direction of numbers to other people, in this case to choreographer Jack Cole. Hawks reportedly was not even on set when Cole staged Marilyn Monroe and Jane Russell's numbers, though presumably he supervised the editor's cutting of the entire film.

Knox's oral history may therefore lead one to wonder who "authors" a studio-era musical. "This study of the making of *An American in Paris*," he concludes in his preface, "reveals the strong possibility, at least in musicals, that the studio was in fact the auteur. No single person made *An American in Paris*; it was a studio creation" (xvi–xvii). There is a great deal of truth to that conclusion, as Kelly and others have long insisted, given the collaborative nature of filmmaking, especially on musicals. Thomas Schatz (2010) and Jerome Christenson (2012) likewise argue that the studios and their producers should be considered the authors of Classical Hollywood films in all genres. Nonetheless, one can still see how a director like Minnelli imprinted his own vision as his films' overriding style, which is to say that, while he did not write the story, create the musical score, or stage the numbers, his imagination made everything in a Minnelli film congeal as a whole. From this perspective, although musicals were achieved in collaboration with the films' stars, choreographers, writers, composers, cinematographers, editors, sound engineers, set designers, and costumers, five names stand out for their innovative achievements, influence, and singular visions: Ernst Lubitsch, Busby Berkeley, Minnelli, Stanley Donen, and Bob Fosse.

Historically but also in terms of his influence, at the top of this short list is **Ernst Lubitsch** (1982–1947). He emigrated to the United States from Germany in 1922. Known as "'the D.W. Griffith of Europe' because of his flair for making large-scale historical spectacles but with a refreshingly modern approach to sexuality" (McBride 2018: 2), Lubitsch had an even more successful and influential career in Hollywood, where he moved from those spectacles to the dramas and comedies for which he became famous in America during the silent era. The "Lubitsch Touch," as it was dubbed and marketed by Paramount, yet also celebrated as an aesthetic standard by subsequent directors like Billy Wilder, describes Lubitsch's witty, evocative, visually sly, and sexually suggestive directorial style. According to Joseph McBride, the Lubitsch Touch "combines characteristic joie de vivre in the actors with an elegant visual design that conveys its meanings largely through sophisticated innuendo" (3). From this perspective, the director's hand is evident in dialogue, the acting and singing, the editing, the sets, even the ensemble dance numbers, which stand out for their sophisticated choreography and camera work.

Lubitsch's first sound film was a musical, *The Love Parade* (1929) with Maurice Chevalier and Jeanette MacDonald. Nominated for six Academy Awards, it was immediately heralded "for its startlingly innovative nature, which pointed the way forward for his colleagues as well as his audiences" in showing how the musical could be more than a revue or backstage story with some songs interspersed in the narrative as show numbers (243). After *The Love Parade* Lubitsch made dramas and comedies while still working in and expanding the musical form: *Monte Carlo* (1930) with MacDonald and Jack Buchanan, *The Smiling Lieutenant* (1931) with Chevalier, Claudette Colbert, and Miriam Hopkins, and *One Hour with You* (1932) with Chevalier and MacDonald. Earlier he had directed segments featuring Chevalier in a revue, *Paramount on Parade* (1930). After making two comedies considered amongst his best work, *Trouble in Paradise* (1932) and *Design for Living* (1933), Lubitsch moved to MGM for a while, where he made *The Merry Widow* with Chevalier and MacDonald. After that musical, which was expensive and did not make back its cost, and feeling he had exhausted what he could do with the genre, Lubitsch did not make another one for fifteen years until his final film, a Betty Grable musical at Twentieth Century-Fox, *The Lady in Ermine* (1948); he died during its production and it was completed by Otto Preminger.

THE LOVE PARADE (1929)

Singing in *The Love Parade* voices the ultimate compatibility of the couple, but their different vocal styles—Chevalier's Parisian cabaret style, MacDonald's trained operatic soprano—also voices the tension that makes for both their sexual frisson and the potential barrier to their happy union. Although Lubitsch was working with the confined camera of early sound, so that visual movement of a scene is achieved through an actor's mobility but mostly through editing (and via some shots filmed without sound to enable the camera to move more flexibly or for extreme long shots), his *Love Parade* is a visually fluid achievement that stands out as being more modern and sophisticated in comparison with other early sound musicals.

The many songs extend the narrative of *The Love Parade*, with Chevalier's numbers first expressing his courtier's libertine attitude towards sex and women and then bemoaning his subordinated status to and emasculation by his Queen once he becomes her Prince Consort; with MacDonald's enacting her sexual desire, first for an abstract "Dream Lover" (a song repeated throughout) and then for her husband; and with their servants (Lupino Lane, Lillian Roth) commenting on and disagreeing about their employers' differences vis-à-vis their social, gender, and political positions (e.g., as wife and husband, man and woman, courtier/Prince Consort and Queen). With their slapstick antics in their numbers (Lane was a trained acrobat), the servants function as a comic Greek chorus observing the marital discord once Chevalier's Count Albert marries MacDonald's Queen Louise of Sylvania, who treats him like a plaything while she carries on affairs of state with her ministers, from which her husband is pointedly excluded.

Figure 5.1 Jeanette MacDonald and Maurice Chevalier in *The Love Parade* (1929, Paramount)

A famous example of the Lubitsch Touch in *The Love Parade* occurs through his witty use of closed doors, which initially prevents the viewer from knowing what is going on in the Queen's bedroom as other characters, ministers, ladies in waiting, and/or servants, who are also outside the inner chamber, witness or speculate, sometimes in song, about what might be happening there. Our curiosity aroused, we are then taken into that room where we are made privy to the intimate conversations and behavior of Louise and Albert during their courtship and marriage.

But there are many other examples that illustrate the director's style as it meshes innuendo with wit and irony. The opening sequence, which encourages us to think that Albert's mistress shoots herself when her husband unexpectedly arrives, turns on itself when we learn that the gun had blanks; what is more, this type of event may have occurred many times previously in Albert's chambers since, after the married couple depart, he drops the gun in a drawer with many revolvers already there. This opening stages the self-dramatization at the heart of these sophisticates' sexual peccadillos. Similarly, when Albert bids adieu to Paris because he has been summoned home due to his scandalous misbehavior as a roué, he sings "Paris, Stay the Same," followed by his servant Jacques (Lane), followed by his dog, who apparently has stolen the hearts of Parisian bitches just as his human has done.

Still another instance of the Lubitsch Touch occurs in the clever way he provides exposition: Lubitsch cuts from Albert in Paris to a touring bus in front of the palace. It bears the banner "See Sylvania First" and the tour guide supplies a brief account of the country's history and its queen. Then we see her being awakened by her ladies in waiting, to whom she will not supply the details of her very erotic dream. Louise simply smiles coquettishly about her "dream lover," which allows one to fill in the sexual details.

Lubitsch's musicals are all fairy tales insofar as they take place in exoticized and imaginary European kingdoms, and this setting gives them greater license for exploring the differential relationship of love and sexuality without fear of censorship. The Chevalier character is typically a Don Juan figure, irresistible to women, none of whom appear to mind his many other conquests; when he falls for the MacDonald character she has to teach him that while "sex" is physical and transient, "love" is more emotional and long-lasting. The Love Parade aligns both Albert's libertine behavior (in "Paris, Stay the Same") and his anger at being emasculated by his marriage (in "Nobody's Using it Now") with the spectator's sympathies by having Chevalier directly face the camera when singing, as if he is taking us into his confidence. At a few other moments he speaks to us in direct address, too.

At the same time, the Lubitsch musicals recognize full well a female's sexuality, which the Chevalier character incites, actualizes, and satisfies. Many examples of the Lubitsch Touch involve the director's wry means of visually suggesting how MacDonald's characters are an equal participant with her lover in the sexual game; even though she may seem to be the voice of moral and social protocols, whereas he views women through a sexist and predatory lens, she is always characterized, often through her facial expressions and body language, as being a very sexual person in her own right, which protocol has repressed. By enabling the female character to act upon and satisfy her desires, the Lubitsch musicals challenge traditional male-female roles, as the servants' song in *The Love Parade*, "The Queen Is Always Right," makes plain. Indeed, the marriage ceremony uniting Alfred and Louise reverses the usual hierarchical gender division for the minister asks him if he is willing to fulfill Her Majesty's every wish, "and to be an obedient and docile husband," so that *he* has to promise to obey *her* "every wish and command," and *she* has to vow to protect *him*. After both say, "I do," they are pronounced "Wife and Man."

The reversal of the man and woman's social and gender status in *The Love Parade* poses problems for Lubitsch's closure, since to achieve the expected Hollywood ending, Queen Louise has to capitulate to her consort's authority as a man or risk unmanning him and sending him away. The problematic of enabling a powerful, authoritative woman like Queen Louise to express and act upon her desires becomes a hallmark of the Lubitsch musical, as do the conservative "happy" endings that work to contain that desire because it threatens patriarchal masculinity. The sympathetic treatment of an emasculated Albert when marriage gives him nothing to do, emphasized by Chevalier's direct address as he complains about it in song, makes the audience more ready to accept Louise's capitulation when she cedes her authority to him—at least in the bedroom. However, one may also read the Lubitsch Touch in its numerous visual manifestations throughout *The Love Parade*, as in all of this director's musicals, as indicating a subtle critique of that type of conciliatory resolution.

If Lubitsch had an immediate successor it was Mark Sandrich (1900–1945), who at RKO produced and directed five musicals starring Fred Astaire and Ginger Rogers: *The Gay Divorcee* (1934), *Top Hat* (1935), *Follow the Fleet* (1936), *Swing Time* (1937), and *Carefree* (1938). At Paramount, Sandrich produced and directed Astaire's teaming with Bing Crosby in *Holiday Inn* (1942) and was preparing *Blue Skies* (1946) with both men when he died. Sandrich was also second-unit director on *Flying Down to Rio* (1933), which first featured Astaire and Rogers. Although these musicals are justly famous for Astaire's innovations in planning his numbers with few edits and in medium to long shots to feature the choreography by following the dancers (for we do know that the star had contractual control over not only his choreography but also how it was to be filmed and cut), Sandrich followed Lubitsch's example in melding the numbers in his musicals as "naturally"—which is to say not as show numbers for the most part— with the narratives. Thus in *Top Hat*, for instance, Astaire worked with Hermes Pan in planning the challenge dance of "Isn't It a Lovely Day (to be Out in the Rain)?" and determined how it was shot and edited, while as the film's producer-director Sandrich saw that the number arose from and moved forward the Astaire-Rogers relationships as narrative action.

In comparison with Lubitsch's musicals and the Astaire-Rogers series, those from **Busby Berkeley** (1895–1976) fit within what Martin Rubin calls a "'Tradition of Spectacle'. ... It is a tradition based on creating feelings of abundance, variety, and wonder" (Rubin 1993: 4). Berkeley began on Broadway where he was dance director on several operettas,

Rodgers and Hart's *A Connecticut Yankee* (1927), the *Earl Carroll Vanities of 1928* (a competitor with the annual *Ziegfeld Follies*), and several revues for the Shuberts. In 1930 he went to Hollywood to stage numbers for producer Samuel Goldwyn's musical comedies with Eddie Cantor: *Whoopee!* (1930), *Palmy Days* (1931), *The Kid from Spain* (1932), and *Roman Scandals* (1933). Moving to Warner Bros, Berkeley became famous for his spectacular numbers in the series of musicals that revived the genre after it had temporarily gone moribund: *42nd Street* (1933), *Gold Diggers of 1933* (1933), *Footloose Parade* (1933), *Wonder Bar* (1934), and *Dames* (1934). In these musicals, as noted in another chapter, Berkeley created and filmed the numbers while someone else directed the narrative scenes. After their success, Warners gave Berkeley control of the entire film at times, beginning with *Gold Diggers of 1935* (1935) with its fourteen-minute number, "Lullaby of Broadway," which functions as a narrative in its own right, and including *Hollywood Hotel* (1937), although he continued to stage numbers for other directors.

By 1939 Berkeley had gone to MGM, where he directed the Mickey Rooney-Judy Garland cycle: *Babes in Arms* (1939), *Strike Up the Band* (1940), and *Babes on Broadway* (1942). After working once more with Garland on *For Me and My Gal* (1942), Berkeley, a hard taskmaster on set who wore his actors down, was fired from the final musical in the Rooney-Garland cycle, *Girl Crazy* (1943) after doing the big "I Got Rhythm" number, and MGM loaned him to Fox for *The Gang's All Here* (1943). Thereafter Berkeley directed or just staged numbers for a host of MGM films, sometimes not receiving a credit for the latter. Toward the end of his career he staged breathtaking water numbers for Esther Williams in *Million Dollar Mermaid* (1952) and *Easy to Love* (1953), and spectacular stunt dance numbers for Bobby Van and Ann Miller in *Small Town Girl* (1953).

Regardless of where and when he worked, Berkeley's musicals are known for several recurring elements, some of which have been touched on already in my previous discussion of "The Shadow Waltz" from *Gold Diggers of 1933*. His numbers are expansive in scope and gigantic in their length. In backstage musicals like the *Gold Digger* series, show numbers begin on a visible and confined stage but quickly enter a visual world of their own with choreography and camera work that makes no pretense of retaining the initial viewpoint of a diegetic spectator. His numbers, too, are often marginal to their narrative settings, whether in terms of their placements (in some musicals, the most spectacular numbers are stacked at the end) or their contexts (show numbers occur without rhyme or reason in plot terms and their entertainment value comes from their spectacle, though at times numbers may pick up themes from the narrative). Berkeley's numbers, furthermore, are well known for their objectification of women since the female ensemble does not dance so much as pose for his camera and overhead shots, whose view fetishizes their bodies, fragmenting and abstracting their human forms into visually compelling, kaleidoscopic patterns. As well as fetishizing the female body in a psychoanalytical sense, Berkeley's numbers treat it as a blatant erotic object in how he films women and as often turns the body into an inhuman object or abstract pattern, as when the chorines form the large violin in "The Shadow Waltz," becoming neon clay, in effect, to the filmmaker's visual sculpting of light and shadow.

THE GANG'S ALL HERE (1943)

The Gang's All Here, Berkeley's first musical in Technicolor, is a jaw-dropping example of his over-the-top visual style in the numbers, his overall direction and filming of stars Alice Faye and Carmen Miranda as well as featured players Edward Everett Horton, Charlotte Greenwood, and Eugene Pallette, and a disinterest in the narrative, especially the romance plot of Faye and minor actor James Ellison, except as it serves to bridge the numbers. Ellison's character speaks cheesy pick-up lines and he deceives Faye about his real identity; upon discovering it, she breaks up with him and their reconciliation is engineered offscreen by his father so the expected happy ending for the couple gets displaced by a series of numbers comprising a show: Benny Goodman and Carmen Miranda's "Peducah," Faye's reprise of "Journey to a Star" with dancing by Sheila Ryan and Tony Demarco, Faye's "Polka Dot Polka" and its big production number, "The Polka Dot Ballet," and another reprise of "Journey to a Star" sung by all the cast except for Ellison.

As Rubin observes, "In some respects, the normal stylistic relationship of numbers and narrative is inverted in *The Gang's All Here*; it is like a musical turned inside out" (164). With the performers' flat delivery of often nonsensical dialogue and scenes that are put together with few edits and are framed like tableaus so that they have a "stage-like quality," Berkeley basically treats the narrative as "sheer spectacle" according to Rubin. As a result, the narrative is integrated to the numbers insofar as it is subordinated to them, and the numbers do not contrast with the narrative so much as intensify its absurdity and potential as spectacle. Numbers have more edits, more dynamic use of space, crane shots, and "eye-popping colors and unearthly decors" (163–164). Even the title makes little sense except as a well-known phrase from a familiar song that plays under the main titles, in contrast, say, with *Meet Me in St. Louis* or *Cover Girl*, titles that summarize a narrative.

Most people remember *The Gang's All Here* for Carmen Miranda's "The Lady in the Tutti Frutti Hat," the number with the big bananas. It begins not with her but with an overhead shot traveling from the orchestra onstage to an organ grinder walking amongst the tables onto the stage, where we see a painted set of banana trees with numerous real-life monkeys climbing through the artificial leaves. The camera moves through the leaves to find barefoot showgirls in peasant costume lying on the ground. They rise to greet Miranda who arrives on a cart stocked with bunches of bananas. Her headdress consists of bananas topped with strawberries that spill down her head and neck to adorn her costume. Her song is self-reflexive: "I wonder why everybody looks at me," she sings, "and then began to talk about a Christmas tree." The lyrics rely on sexual innuendo: Miranda is the titular lady in the hat who dresses so gaily because she feels so gay ("and what's wrong with that?"); she says "yes" when asked out on dates by "Americanos" but refuses to take off her "high hat" to kiss a guy because, if she ever took it off, then "*ay, ay,*" she sings with a wink to the spectator; but she did that once for Johnny Smith and he was "very happy." The showgirls repeat a chorus about Miranda feeling "so gay" and encircle her in a xylophone made of bananas, which she plays.

Miranda disappears as we see the showgirls on the beach in front of giant strawberries; they each hold a giant banana, which they move up and down in precise synchronization to form a canopy. In an overhead shot as a chorus hums the melody, half a dozen women lie on the ground holding giant strawberries over their heads like a beachball, while the rest wave their giant phallic bananas up and down, the image evoking a flower opening and closing to be fertilized. The showgirls leave to do more patterns with the bananas, finally forming a canopied avenue with the giant bananas, as Miranda returns, singing a new verse about "Brazilian senoritas" who "play together" during the day, "But when the topical moon is in the sky," then "*ay, ay,* they have a different kind of time." And even she forgets the time, she adds, as her cart is wheeled away and the showgirls all wave goodbye. With that suggestion of the women engaging in sexual activity with each other (for the only men on the island are the band and two muscle men who accompany the cart carrying Miranda), the number returns to the nightclub stage and the organ grinder, where he is joined by eleven other organ grinders, each with a live monkey. Miranda repeats the song's chorus in medium shot, and as the camera slowly moves away we see she is standing in front of a painted backdrop, with giant strawberries to her right and left to imply a drawn perspective and a plume of bananas seeming to rise from her headdress. The final long shot reveals the stage as the curtain descends upon her figure.

Figure 5.2 Carmen Miranda as "The Lady in the Tutti Frutti Hat" in *The Gang's All Here* (1943, Twentieth Century-Fox)

Figure 5.3 Showgirls raise and lower giant bananas in "The Lady in the Tutti Frutti Hat" in *The Gang's All Here* (1943, Twentieth Century-Fox)

"The Lady in the Tutti Frutti Hat" has all the elements of a Berkeleyesque production number—the collapsing of naturalistic space into pure cinematic spectacle, the fetishizing of showgirls who are not dancers but figures that comprise vivid and compelling visual patterns, the theme of rampant sexuality, all with the addition of Carmen Miranda and her carnivalesque appearance, which supplies the subject matter of the song. The number, in short, is all about Miranda's star image but also about fecundity.

But "Tutti Frutti Hat" is topped by the finale, "The Polka Dot Polka" and the ballet. Boys and girls wearing polka dots dance the polka as Alice Faye walks among them, singing about this dance, a popular mode of courtship back in the 1880s. Though the children begin by singing with her in their own voices, they are eventually dubbed by an adult chorus which they mime. The song concludes with Faye first observing, "the thing that led to love / was her polka-dotted glove," but then noting that the dance has since become "passé" although "the polka dot lives on" in an assortment of clothing such as "parasols and shirts / and bathing suits and skirts" while "the gentlemen still love / a polka-dotted glove."

Now as the ballet begins the number becomes surreal, a visual festival of abstract shapes and animation inspired by the polka dot. The image of a polka-dotted sleeve and woman's hand yields red neon hoops against a black background, the camera traveling around them until it focuses on a single hoop which then appears to drop through space, passing numerous other hoops. As the camera moves beneath the hoops, the silhouettes of showgirls start to become visible. They stretch their arms and catch the hoops as they descend toward them; the frame becomes better illuminated as the women, dressed like star fleet commanders (as a student of mine once commented), slowly rotate the hoops in a circular motion. Moving back, the camera reveals the women lined up on several ascending platforms, with the gigantic shadow of one showgirl looming behind them. The screen darkens and a single hoop moves toward center frame; it becomes solid, filling up the screen until we see the women seated on a platform, itself decked out with polka dots, each holding a giant pink disc. Standing, they hold the discs in front of their bodies and above their heads; turning around, they reveal the discs' green underside. Placing the discs on the platform edge, the women follow the objects as they begin to move toward the camera. With a dissolve from a closeup of the disc back to the women standing on the platform, the women hold out their arms as the discs, now orange on one side and grey on the other, rise to them from the ground (in a shot that was printed in reverse); then each row of women pass the discs to the row beneath them, and so on.

Finally, one of the orange discs fills the screen and behind it we see Alice Faye's face, her body wrapped in a blue, shiny, swirling cloth. The image splits with multiple views of Faye as if viewed through a kaleidoscope. The camera moves back so that we see the kaleidoscopic view as a circle highlighted by the black screen. The kaleidoscopic image twists and turns as Faye's head becomes less discernible except as a blot of color against the shiny blue cloth; then it disappears entirely as the image becomes an abstract design inspired by the figure of a showgirl moving her arms up and down as the kaleidoscopic image changes, becoming a moveable display of vibrant colors—blues, reds, oranges, purples—and shapes barely evocative of the showgirls holding the discs moving to and from the camera.

Figure 5.4 Alice Faye sings "The Polka Dot Polka" in *The Gang's All Here* (1943, Twentieth Century-Fox)

Figure 5.5 Alice Faye at the end of the polka dot number in *The Gang's All Here* (1943, Twentieth Century-Fox)

As the orchestra reverts back to the melody of "Journey to a Star," the cast's heads appear in a circle, each actor appearing individually in boy-girl fashion, and each singing two lines of the verse. Faye appears last, completing the verse, and then the heads return, this time against a cobalt blue background; Faye winks as Ellison, who did not have a solo, joins her. The heads of the full ensemble appear in bottom frame and everyone repeats the verse together. A curtain of spraying water rises upward from the bottom of the screen to signal "The End" of *The Gang's All Here*.

More so than "The Lady in the Tutti Frutti Hat," the polka dot number begins referentially; however absurd, the lyrics are about a real dance in a real time period, and the polka dot itself is a real clothes pattern. However, once the song concludes, the number ceases to be illusionistic. The production design and the showgirls' actions make no referential sense—which is why my student felt the need to supply a referent for the costume from a sci-fi TV series—except as something fascinating to watch onscreen. When Faye returns in the number's kaleidoscopic finale, any pretense of representation goes away entirely and at that moment what we have is pure, swirling, undulating colors—imagery that vacates any semblance of representational meaning but signifies the camera's empowerment, its mobility and visuality, as cinema.

Like Lubitsch and Berkeley, **Vincente Minnelli** (1903–1996) directed musicals under studio conditions. Making full use of the specialized talent behind as well as in front of the camera at MGM, as a director he is known as a superb stylist, with particular attention paid to his camera work, color and composition, and mise-en-scene.

As noted already, Knox's book details what the many people who helped to create Minnelli's *An American in Paris* did on that production—from Kelly's staging and filming of the choreography to Alan Jay Lerner's screenplay, Irene Sharaff's designs and costumes for the ballet,

Adrienne Fazan's editing, Alfred Gilks and John Alton's cinematography and lighting, Keogh Gleason's sets, Preston Ames's art direction, and Saul Chaplin's, John Green's, and Conrad Salinger's scoring and arrangements of George Gershwin's music—but Minnelli directed the entire film. As Lerner recalled, Minnelli told him what he needed dramatically. "With the script finished, I turned it over to Vincente, who was, of course, responsible for making it come alive. After all, it was still type on a page" (Knox 1973: 42). "When Vincente is at his best," Lerner also stated, "his pictures have a look, a patina, that nobody else has ever achieved in motion pictures. He is as unique as Lubitsch was in his way" (21). Kelly, too, stated that, while he himself staged and chose the camera angles for the seventeen-minute ballet (and he, Sharaff, Gleason, Ames, and the rest planned it under Minnelli's eye while the director filmed a quickie movie, *Father's Little Dividend* [1951]), Minnelli was on set during its production, watching and making it "come alive" with that particular "look." As Kelly recalled:

His eye, his experience, is just invaluable. Nobody does a musical alone. Nobody! Minnelli's eye for color is the great thing. I don't think you can find a better costume designer in the world than Irene Sharaff, but, when you get all the choreography done and get everybody on the stage floor, you can always find that Minnelli will have some way to adjust the color so that we'll have a better composition. ...Vincent was able to polish it even more.

(165–166)

The Minnelli "look" began with his job as a window dresser for a leading department store in Chicago, which led to work supervising costumes and sets for stage shows and musicals in New York City. Though he had an unhappy six-month stint at Paramount in 1937, several years later Arthur Freed at MGM persuaded him to try Hollywood again. After assisting on numbers in several musicals directed by others, Minnelli directed for Freed *Cabin in the Sky* (1943), an all African-American musical with Lena Horne and Ethel Waters, and *Meet Me in St. Louis* (1944), which began his association with Judy Garland and cemented his importance to the Freed unit. After *St. Louis* the pair did her numbers in *Ziegfeld Follies* (1946) and *Til the Clouds Roll By* (1946), the nonmusical *The Clock* (1946), and *The Pirate* (1948). They married in 1945, had their daughter Liza, but then their relationship became turbulent, and they divorced a few years later. By then, too, Minnelli was working with other stars (Fred Astaire in *Yolanda and the Thief* [1945], Kelly in *The Pirate*) and other genres too. In the 1950s, he was as well known for his explosive melodramas (*The Bad and the Beautiful* [1952], *The Cobweb* [1954], *Tea and* Sympathy [1956], *Lust for Life* [1956], *Some Came Running* [1958]) and domestic comedies (*Father of the Bride* [1950], *The Long, Long Trailer* [1954], *Designing Woman* [1957]) as for his many musicals (*An American in Paris*, *The Band Wagon* [1953], *Brigadoon* [1954], *Kismet* [1955], *Gigi* [1958]).

The Minnelli filmography is, first of all, noted for the bold colors and intricate production design that distinguish his films. At the studio everyone knew about Minnelli's voluminous library of research books and clipping files from which he drew inspiration for sets and costumes, which he then handed to the appropriate departments to execute. *Paris*, for instance, with the exception of some brief second-unit photography, was shot entirely at the studio, which required construction of the elaborate and generally realistic café and surrounding streets and the river bank settings that center the book scenes along with the half-a-dozen more unworldly locations for the ballet, all inspired by images in Minnelli's files. The ballet famously draws on the paintings of Impressionist and Post-Impressionist artists—Dufy, Renoir, Rousseau, Van Gogh, and Toulouse-Lautrec.

Similarly, it "was Vincente's brain child" according to Sharaff (Knox 1973: 134), who also did the costumes for the sequence introducing Leslie Caron in a variety of moods as she dances to "Embraceable You," to clothe the actress in a vivid color in contrast to a monochromatic setting with period furniture, the designs of each differentiated according to the dance style (a Jacobean set, a Biedermeier set, a Baroque set, and so forth). Likewise, in *The Band Wagon* Minnelli visualizes but without yet commenting on the difference between the older show-biz dancer played by Astaire (in a black formal suit) and the younger classic ballerina played by Cyd Charisse (in a black cocktail dress) who have not yet met, by having each set against a differently colored space while waiting for the backers' audition to conclude, with him and his partners, Oscar Levant and Nanette Fabray, in a yellow room and her and her mentor, James Mitchell, in a red one. The entrance hall is lavender. And each room is filled out with details that mate with the particular decor—potted plants, paintings, bric-a-brac, tasteful furniture, bookcases, ornate lamps, and so forth. Cutting back and forth between the two rooms, as each dancer expresses anxiety about working with the other, Minnelli uses the vivid chromatic contrast to visualize their two distinct worlds—and their contrary views with respect to dance.

Enhancing the Minnelli "look" is the camerawork, his many dazzling overhead and tracking shots in particular. Alone among his many fellow directors at MGM, Minnelli was given greater license to request the expensive crane equipment because of the finesse and care with which he used it. He often used this for a sweeping overview of a setting, which made for viewer appreciation of the realistic detail that went into the creation of an often fabulous locale. Riding the crane, he supervised the finale of "'S Wonderful, 'S Marvelous" in *An American in Paris*, for instance. In the film Kelly and friend Georges Guetary are both in love with Caron, and each thinks she returns his passion equally. The song expresses the delight the two men feel in being in love with her. After they sing the chorus in the café, the men move to the street outside; Guetary continues vocalizing while Kelly taps accompaniment until they again sing together. Then Guetary leans against a pole, whistling the tune, while Kelly taps around him. All of this is done first with a medium shot in the café, then with a long shot to show their full bodies when they are outside. With a cut to an angled shot, the men shake hands and go their separate ways, still singing. As the camera moves progressively back from their figures, Minnelli's tracking crane shot shows more of the street and the many observers, along with the flower stall, fruit cart, cars, and a van. The number concludes with Kelly at the top far right of the frame and Guetary at the bottom far left of it, with the teeming street life of Paris between them.

Minnelli's films are further characterized by a fascination with artists, performers, or dreamers, not surprising since many of the people who worked with him on *American in Paris* referred to him as a "dreamer" himself. His musicals tend to feature big fantasy production numbers (or, as a variation, the extended show-within-a show in *The Band Wagon*) that is as other-worldly in its décor and costuming as Berkeley's though consistently identifiable as Minnelli's. The *American in Paris* ballet exemplifies his interest in artists and their dreaming, to be sure—Kelly plays a painter and the ballet, his fantasy, simultaneously choreographs the allure of Paris for his art and his feelings for Caron, who keeps appearing and disappearing in each new section with its shift to a new, painterly-inspired setting and costuming—but one finds this theme visualized in many of Minnelli's other musicals too. Brigadoon is an imaginary place in Scotland that comes alive every hundred years. *Kismet* takes place in a fairy-tale kingdom set in ancient Bagdad, while the earlier *Yolanda and the Thief* and *The Pirate* happen in fictionalized Latin American countries with exotic landscapes and colorful, other-worldly costuming. *Yolanda* finds Astaire playing a confidence man whom the virginal Lucille Bremer believes is her Guardian Angel. The set piece is Astaire's dream number, "Will You Marry Me?" His dream reveals his anxious sense of being ensnared by his scheme, and the costumes and décor in it anticipate what Minnelli does with the *Paris* ballet.

The Pirate is perhaps the perfect expression of Minnelli's concern with dreamers and performers. Judy Garland's Manuela is infatuated with the legend of the pirate Macoco while the itinerant actor, Gene Kelly's Serafin, pretends to be the man of her dreams in order to woo her. He discovers her passion when he hypnotizes her as part of his show, which results in her rousing "Mack the Black" number and later

Figure 5.6 The conclusion of "'S Wonderful, 'S Marvelous" in *An American in Paris* (1951, MGM)

in her daydream fantasy of Serafin as the pirate in the erotic "Pirate Ballet." Manuela does fall in love with Serafin when she realizes that her betrothed, the boring mayor of the village (Walter Slezak), is the real Mack the Black in hiding. At the end, the couple go on the road as clown performers ("Be a Clown"), which satisfies Manuela's initial longing to see the world, the source of her infatuation with Macoco's legend in the first place.

THE BAND WAGON (1953)

The Band Wagon, Minnelli's only backstage musical, similarly uses theater as a metaphor for dreaming. Fred Astaire plays Tony Hunter, a mature dancer whose Hollywood career has stalled and is hoping for a comeback in a new Broadway musical with a book and score written by his friends, Lily and Lester Marton (Nanette Fabray, Oscar Levant) about a children's book writer who makes his living by writing lurid detective novels under an alias. The tune, "That's Entertainment," which became MGM's theme song, celebrates how all art, high and low, elite and popular, is simply entertainment; furthermore, the lyrics could well be a Minnelli mantra: "The world is a show / the show is a world / of entertainment!" However, that message gets momentarily forgotten as production of "The Band Wagon" gets underway. The Martons hire the esteemed director, Jeffrey Cordova (Jack Buchanan), who turns the light-hearted musical into a new and more heavyweight (not to say more pretentious) version of Faust and casts the younger ballet star Gabrielle Gerard (Cyd Charisse) opposite Tony with her mentor Paul Byrd (James Mitchell) signed to choreograph. This situation immediately sets up a dual focus by portraying Tony and Gaby as opposites in terms of their gender (male/female), their dance styles (tap/ ballet), their backgrounds (popular/classical), and their ages (older/younger).

The first hour or so of The Band Wagon concerns the hard work of putting together a musical as Cordova's "Band Wagon" never gets off the ground, losing its entertainment value. Unable to keep up with the balletic staging of the dancing by Byrd, Tony's numbers get cut; he and Gaby do not get along and snipe at each other during rehearsals; Cordova's elaborate staging repeatedly has troubles due to the heavy, elaborate scenery, stalled turntables, and unreliable special effects machinery; and the bickering Martons refuse to speak to each other. During all this tumult, Tony and Gaby reconcile by discovering they can indeed dance together when they leave the theater and find themselves in Central Park. Their duet, "Dancing in the Dark," is an elegant demonstration of their suitability as dancers and future lovers.

Predictably, Cordova's version bombs terribly in New Haven and the backers all flee after the curtain falls. Tony then takes command; he restores the Martons' original light-hearted conception of the story and sells his own collection of Impressionist paintings to refinance the production in order to extend its tryout run in additional cities prior to opening in New York. What follows is a sequence of numbers featuring Astaire, Charise, Buchanan, and Fabray in joyful singing and dancing, concluding with "The Girl Hunt Ballet." As predictably, Tony's "Band Wagon" is a big hit on opening night. At the opening night party, the five stars sing a reprise of "That's Entertainment" and Gaby makes explicit the correlation of the couple and the show when she says, "The show's a big hit, Tony. It's going to run a long time. As far as I'm concerned, it's going to run forever."

"The Girl Hunt Ballet" functions as the dream ballets do in other Minnelli musicals. It has fun parodying the popular Mickey Spillane thrillers and, like a Busby Berkeley number, in its multiple sets and camera angles, not to say the running voice-over narration by Astaire, it exceeds the spatial realism of the legitimate theater stage where it supposedly takes place. This "impossible" number takes aim at paperback thrillers, which inspired the premise of the show-within-the film in the first place, with their hard, tough, and brawny male detectives and the misogyny and violence that motivate their plots. Charisse plays two roles—the blonde ballerina-type in blue chiffon and toe shoes who turns out to be the villain and the brunette femme fatale in a slinky red dress and with long legs that wrap around Astaire when they dance. Astaire goes off with the brunette at the end, saying, in mock tough-guy prose, "She was bad. She was dangerous. I wouldn't trust her any farther than I could throw her. But—she was my kind of woman." The ballet's story thus reverses expectations insofar as the femme fatale is "bad" and "dangerous" but innocent of deceiving Astaire whereas the vulnerable blonde turns out to be "Mr. Big." Moreover, Astaire's lithe and slender body belies his age and his "tough" voiceover as he moves gracefully and effortlessly through the various dance sections, projecting an alternate expression of masculinity, just as the gangsters all do balletic leaps and slides while shooting each other. The doubling of Charisse in the number, finally, along with the blonde's seeming vulnerability but ultimate duplicity, restages and resolves Tony's own uncertainty about Gaby's suitability as a dance partner and lover given their contrasting styles, backgrounds, and ages.

Figure 5.7 "She was bad. She was dangerous." Cyd Charisse and Fred Astaire in "The Girl Hunt Ballet" in *The Band Wagon* (1953, MGM)

As further evidence of Minnelli's hand despite Kidd's and Astaire's collaboration on the choreography, "The Girl Hunt Ballet" successfully uses every stage device (such as smoke machines) and dance tropes (such as ballet lifts, jumps, kicks, and splits) that Cordova and Byrd had mishandled in the first

"Band Wagon," which Minnelli satirized as inauthentic "high art" in contrast with the "popular art" that Tony's revised "Band Wagon" celebrates. If the first version is bloated and overdone in all respects, the second one is exciting to watch in its complex execution. For that matter, *The Band Wagon* may be viewed as the director's riposte to those film reviewers who had criticized the ballet in *An American in Paris* for being "less interesting, less imaginative, less inventive than the ballet of *Red Shoes*[, a British dance musical from 1948 that was an enormous hit in the United States and popularized ballet classes for young women], from which it clearly derives" (quoted in Knox 1973: 183). The eight Academy Awards won by *American in Paris* refuted that critique, to be sure. Yet while *Paris* won Best Picture, Minnelli lost the directing prize. He finally did win for directing *Gigi* (1958), the second Minnelli musical to sweep the Oscars, and some think that award was belated recognition of his achievement in *An American in Paris*—and possibly *The Band Wagon* as well.

Whereas Minnelli's signature could be found in his camera work and mise-en-scene, his colleague at MGM, **Stanley Donen** (1924–2019), is remembered for his imaginative and innovative special effects and use of the new widescreen. Leaving his home state of South Carolina for New York City as a teen, Donen worked as a dancer in the chorus of two musicals with Gene Kelly, *Pal Joey* (1940–1941), which was Kelly's star-making performance on the boards, and *Best Foot Forward* (1941–1942), which Kelly choreographed. Making his way to Hollywood, Donen helped stage numbers and danced in the chorus of MGM's film version of *Best Foot Forward* (1943). Kelly then asked him to help film the "alter ego" dance in *Cover Girl* (1944). The film's director, Charles Vidor, thought having Kelly dance with himself would be impossible, but Donen, who had been fascinated with cameras since his childhood, said he knew how to do it. According to his interview in *Private Screenings* (first cablecast in the United States on Turner Classic Movies on 6

December 2006), Donen directed the sequence, methodically counting off the beats and marking the camera's movement on the floor to insure the synchronicity of Kelly's dancing twice, once before the cameras as his character and a second time, with the first dance blacked out to double expose the negative, as the ghostly alter-ego.

Donen subsequently staged dance numbers for several of Columbia's low-budget musicals but returned to MGM after a year. He again worked with Kelly on his dancing duet with the animated Jerry the Mouse in *Anchors Aweigh* (1945), the idea for which he takes credit in his TCM interview, and he staged numbers for big budget musicals such as *Holiday in Mexico* (1946) and *This Time for Keeps* (1947). Donen codirected Kelly's numbers in *Living in a Big Way* (1947) and *Take Me Out to the Ball Game* (1949), for which they wrote the story and which served as a tryout for their first co-directing assignment, *On the Town* (1949). Thereafter they codirected *Singin' in the Rain* (1952) and *It's Always Fair Weather* (1955). Who did what in the Kelly-Donen collaboration has always been somewhat controversial, with accounts varying, but in his archival history of the Freed unit's musicals, Hugh Fordin states that, when making *On the Town*, "Kelly and Donen rehearsed on two adjacent rehearsal halls. They would bounce back and forth from one to the other, showing each other what they were doing" (Fordin 1984: 261). Fordin also describes how they split their work when making *Singin' in the Rain*, with Kelly shooting on one sound stage and Donen on another. "That was a marvelous kind of interdependence and independence we had with each other," Kelly recalled (358). However, shooting on their third film, *It's Always Fair Weather*, became acrimonious for reasons never made clear and the Kelly-Donen collaboration ended after that musical.

One can see Donen's hand in the two special-effects numbers he did with Kelly, whose star presence meant that he received most of the credit while his collaborator was treated as an invisible assistant, because all sorts of innovative camera work distinguish Donen's subsequent career once he started directing on his own. (Kelly's own solo-directing projects are less distinguished.) Donen's innovations are impressive because they were not done with computers but replied upon his knowing how to manipulate cinematic technologies like double-exposure, the size of the film frame, and montage.

The opening of *On the Town* features a montage of Kelly, Frank Sinatra, and Jules Munshin singing "New York, New York" in real locations around the city, beginning at the Brooklyn Navy Yard and traveling to the Italian, Chinese, and Jewish sections, the Staten Island Ferry and Statue of Liberty, the Third Avenue L, Washington Square, Grant's Tomb, Central Park on horseback, bicycles, and foot, atop a two-decker bus, the roof of Rockefeller Center and ending in front of the Prometheus sculpture at ground level. Fordin describes how the continuity had to be well planned "like mosaic pieces which had to fit a certain portion of the prerecorded music track" (264), which is also to say that the sequence was cut together to the music as a montage, much as Donen had planned the "alter ego" dance by rigorously counting and keeping to the beats. The mosaic-like nature of the sequence, however, is somewhat illusory as most of the location shots are fleeting, lasting only a few moments, as the orchestra plays "New York, New York" on the soundtrack; at only a few stops do the performers stop and sing: at the navy yard, on the ferry and in front of the statue, on top of Rockefeller Center and in front of Prometheus, behind which one can still scores of locals and tourists watching the filming.

On his own, Donen did something a bit more complicated when filming *Funny Face* (1957) on location in Paris. In a single edited sequence, Fred Astaire, Audrey Hepburn, and Kay Thompson each sing parts of "Bonjour, Paris!" individually at different landmarks of the French capital—this number did have to time every "mosaic piece" of the stars' individual singing snatches of the song so that the bits and pieces all fit together in synchrony with the prerecorded track. But Donen's expertise with montage is evident throughout *Funny Face*, a musical about fashion photography. During Thompson's "Think Pink" number he inserts a montage of fashion models all in pink to illustrate the campy lyrics sung by an offscreen female chorus ("Drive in pink / Come alive in pink / Have a dive in pink!"). With shots of a model diving as we hear those lyrics, Donen divides the screen to show her in different poses and momentarily freezes the images, one after the other, to simulate photographs. That trick then supplies the visual trope later on when Astaire, playing a character modeled on famed photographer Richard Avedon, does a fashion shoot with Hepburn at famous Parisian landmarks. Astaire creates a scenario for Hepburn's pose and, after he clicks his camera, the image freezes. For each still image Donen does something different, blanching the color to visualize a negative, drenching the image in a single color, or changing its shape inside the black cinematic frame.

A variation of special visual effects to enhance a number also happens in the earlier *Give a Girl a Break* (1953), when Bob Fosse daydreams about Debbie Reynolds in a reprise of their earlier song, "In Our United State." Here, in printing the sequence, Donen reverses some sections of the couple's dancing so that snow goes up instead of falling down, Fosse and Reynolds dance up a staircase backwards, and inflated balloons appear at their fingertips instead of being popped, although at other points in the number the couple do pop balloons, do dance down those same stairs, and snow does fall normally.

Donen's first solo directing assignment was *Royal Wedding* (1950) and here his innovativeness is justly famous. In "You're All the World to Me" a joyous, love-happy Astaire dances on the walls and ceiling of his hotel room. Staging the number this way was "obvious," Donen explained in his TCM interview, because "of all the people on earth, Fred Astaire seems the least affected by gravity." It was done with a revolving set, a room inside a wheel, with the camera and everything in the room nailed down, and the camera operator strapped to the floor on his belly. As the wheel turned, it looked like Astaire was defying gravity with his dancing. Because his star had rehearsed this number for several weeks, getting comfortable with the rotating room as he danced, Donen recalls that he was able to film it in ninety minutes with minimal cuts in order to sustain the illusion of Astaire's gravity-free dancing. (Donen repeated this effect when he directed Lionel Ritchie in the music video, "Dancing on the Ceiling" [1986]).

Another Donen specialty in his musicals is his use of split screens. In the opening sequence of *Give a Girl a Break* five wannabe stars of varying abilities sing the title number with one woman in the middle and two on each side, a configuration repeated in *Damn Yankees* (1958) when half a dozen wives agree that "Six Months Out of Every Year" they lose their husbands to baseball. Similarly, in *Funny Face* the montage in "Think Pink" uses split screens and "Bonjour, Paris!" reaches its conclusion when Hepburn, Astaire, and Thompson, each alone in a different Paris locale, realize in split screen that something is still missing from their touring and all three end up at the Eifel Tower.

Donen's most elaborate use of split screen takes advantage of CinemaScope's extreme width in *It's Always Fair Weather*, planned as a kind of follow-up to *On the Town* in addressing the disillusionment of GIs a decade after returning home from fighting in World War II. The widescreen process allowed for splitting the screen equally in three sections, in contrast with the more compacted Academy screen ratios of the other examples, including the somewhat wider VistaVision shape of *Funny Face*. In *Fair Weather* a montage takes the ex-GIs from the high spirits and exuberance of their street dancing right after they return home ("March, March" and "Time for Parting") to the present day, with Kelly, Dan Dailey, and Michael Kidd (the choreographer in one of his few film roles) each displayed year by year in a section of the screen, their lives becoming more conformist (for Dailey, an adman, and Kidd, a cook) and more self-indulgent and disreputable (for Kelly, a gambler and ladies' man). Later in the film, in "Once Upon a Time," the three men reflect upon their dashed dreams; each man appears in a different space while doing a soft shoe dance, their footwork in perfect synchronization. In fact, only with their hands do their movements sometimes not mesh perfectly; for instance, at one point, when the choreography has the men punch a fist into their other hand, Dailey's gesture is several seconds ahead of Kelly's and Kidd's.

Leaving MGM in 1957, Donen expanded his talents to other genres, romantic comedies like *Indiscreet* (1958) and thrillers like *Charade* (1963)

Figure 5.8 Dan Dailey, Gene Kelly, and Michael Kidd dance in split screen to "Once Upon a Time" in *It's Always Fair Weather* (1955, MGM)

in particular, eventually leaving musicals behind after *Damn Yankees*. He returned to the genre twice in later years, first with the unsuccessful *Little Prince* (1974) and then in the second half of *Movie Movie* (1978), a pastiche making gentle fun of Warners films genres of 1933, a boxer story and a musical. But Donen was always known mostly for his musicals, as his recent obituaries recall. When accepting his honorary Academy Award in 1998, Donen sang "Cheek to Cheek" to his Oscar and then danced, as the audience applauded wildly.

SEVEN BRIDES FOR SEVEN BROTHERS (1954)

Donen's most popular musical was the critically acclaimed *Seven Brides for Seven Brothers* (1954), which makes full use of the CinemaScope frame in his filming of dance numbers. As he would subsequently be able to do when he made parts of *Funny Face* in Paris, Donen had wanted to film *Seven Brides*, a Western musical taking place in Oregon Territory in 1850, on location in the Northwest, but MGM would not agree, forcing him to do the musical entirely on the backlot with second-unit footage for one or two brief sequences. This explains the artificial look of *Seven Brides* in its outdoor scenes. Furthermore, with CinemaScope a relatively new process, Donen had to shoot two versions of his musical, one in 'Scope and one with different staging in "flat" (the square Academy ratio to be masked for pseudo-widescreen exhibition). As far as Donen was concerned, with so many dancers featured at once in Michael Kidd's choreography, wide-screen was the only way to go, and he was right. You might notice how numbers comprise many long takes to keep all the dancers in the frame. The alternate version, which used up a quarter of his budget and for which Donen had to readjust his camerawork so that all the dancers remained visible, ended up never being shown in theatres, though it is now available as an extra on the DVD and Blu-ray.

Donen was luckier with getting an original score for the film, resisting the inclination of producer Jack Cummings to use traditional folk songs. The score by Gene de Paul and Johnny Mercer perfectly structures the musical according to the genre's conventional male-female dual focus, which here juxtaposes femininity, domesticity, refinement, and courtship against masculinity, barbarousness, coarseness, and abduction. As Adam, Howard Keel's "Bless Your Beautiful Hide" recounts his desire to find a wife for cooking, cleaning, and taking care of him and his six brothers, and it is counterpointed by Jane Powell's "Wonderful, Wonderful Day," which expresses the joy and hope felt by her character, Milly, once she marries Adam. Soon realizing that a wife is just a glorified servant in Adam's eyes, Milly tries to make appreciate him what she feels for him in "When You're in Love," a number Adam subsequently reprises to one of his brothers as his feelings for Milly deepen. In "Goin' Co'tin'" Milly teaches the brothers how to court women and to dance, preparing for the spirited dancing in the barn-raising sequence, and this number has its match in Adam's "Sobbin' Women" when he uses Plutarch's story of the rape of the Sabine women to inspire the brothers to kidnap the women they have each fallen for. In between those numbers the brothers sing "Lonesome Polecat" to express their listlessness for missing the women, which in turn is balanced by the women singing "June Bride" as they are confined to the big farmhouse after an avalanche prevents their rescue. In the final number, the brothers and their prospective brides together sing "Spring, Spring, Spring" as the snow melts, the men have learned how better to treat the women, and the couples celebrate nature's renewal after the harsh winter. The progression of numbers indicates how *Seven Brides for Seven Brothers* frames its narrative, which tames sexual heat by turning it into romantic love, through the annual cycle of seasonal rebirth and reproduction common to farm life on the frontier.

Today, *Seven Brides for Seven Brothers* may seem dated, even objectionable, in its premise of the brothers kidnapping the women for brides, thereby taking them without their consent—despite the fact that, beforehand, they have seemed to favor the brothers during the barn-raising dance. Moreover, during the "Spring" number, as the men and women witness farm animal births and the growth of new greenery, the women fall back in love with their kidnappers—to the point that when the mountain pass clears they refuse to go home. So it is worth remembering that *Seven Brides* rebukes Adam and his siblings for their brutishness as men. Milly is a strong, assertive female who not only tames the brothers upon her arrival, getting them to shave, wear clean clothes, eat properly, and dance, but she also chastises all seven men for their actions. "What kind of men are you anyway?" she exclaims when they arrive after carrying off the women from their families in town. "Are you animals that you would do a thing like this?" And she throws the men out of the house and into the barn for the winter's duration until the snow thaws and the women can return home. Indeed, like many melodramas and comedies of the 1950s, *Seven Brides for Seven Brothers* addresses the problematics of an aggressive, predatory form of masculinity in postwar American, which is the historical context for better appreciating what its narrative does to this kidnapping narrative. Thus what redeems Adam is fatherhood, since the birth of his daughter is what changes his view of women as the property of men.

An additional factor mitigating the kidnapping narrative is the great dancing in the numbers, which characterizes the brothers in terms of their physical grace and fluency, belying the supposed brutishness of their characters in the plot. For another fight that Donen won with Cummings was hiring ballet dancers Matt Maddox, Marc Platt, Tommy Rall, and Jacques D'Ambroise for four of the brothers. (Aside from Keel, the other brothers are played by gymnast Russ Tramblyn, whose expertise is worked into the choreography, and MGM contract player Jeff Richards, who was not a dancer.) As Donen recalled, "The studio said to me, 'You can't be serious, you're going to make a picture about backwoodsmen with people from the Ballet Theater, what are you going to have, pansy backwoodsmen?'" (Harvey 1973: 6). But the director countered that dancing is a masculine activity, as Michael Kidd's "muscular" choreography proves in terms of how it uses the considerable physical expertise and agility of the dancers in some daring moves that rival professional stunt work in action movies.

Three dance numbers stand out in this regard. The most famous is the barn-raising dance when the brothers compete with their town rivals to woo the women as prospective partners. As well as doing traditional folk dancing steps with the women, who alternate between them and their town beaus, the brothers do somersaults, slides, stand on their hands, and leap in the air and over the backs of their rivals. Maddox, Rall, Tamblyn, and Platt each show off in competition dancing with the townsmen, dancing on the turning crank of a well, on a long plank of wood, with an ax, even while arm wrestling. Donen's camera keeps everyone in the frame for relatively long periods during this number, too; even when he cuts to a medium shot of some dancers, Donen almost immediately tracks backward to capture the entire ensemble of six women and twelve men.

Figure 5.9 The barn-raising dance in *Seven Brides for Seven Brothers* (1954, MGM)

The other two dance numbers that stand out are "Goin' Co'tin'," which almost magically effects the transformation of the brutish brothers into polished dancers as Milly teaches them how to dance, preparing for the barn-raising number and contrasting with Adam's "Sobbin' Women," and "Lonesome Polecat," in which the brothers go through the motions of working outside in the snow while pining for the women. Donen shot this latter number in one long take; given the complex staging, captured by the camera as it moves from and among varying configurations of the brothers, this meant that all six men had repeatedly to hit their marks perfectly as they sang, danced their trance-like movements, and chopped wood for the winter. The intricacy of the staging and camera movement during this long take, which can go without notice, is as impressive as other more famous long takes, such as the openings of *Touch of Evil* (1958) and *The Player* (1992).

Throughout his career, **Bob Fosse** (1927–1987) alternated between stage and screen. As a teen he played in vaudeville and bur-lesque houses, eventually creating an act with his first wife, and as a young man went to Hollywood where he danced in several MGM musicals: *Give a Girl a Break* (1953), *The Affairs of Dobie Gillis* (1953), and *Kiss Me Kate* (1953), for which, without receiving screen credit, he staged a minute of his dancing with Carol Haney—"a jazz Apache dance in miniature" (Winkler 2018: 33)—as part of the number, "From this Moment On." He received screen credit for the chore-ography of Columbia's *My Sister Eileen* (1955), the highlight of which is his bravura challenge dance with Tommy Rall that exploits their different styles and training as each man tries to out-dance the other, ending in a draw.

Leaving Hollywood, Fosse returned to New York, where he choreographed *The Pajama Game* (1954–1956) and *Damn Yankees* (1955–1957), repeating this assignment when each was filmed by codirectors Stanley Donen and George Abbot, two of Fosse's mentors, in 1956 and 1957, respectively. For "Who's Got the Pain" in *Damn Yankees* Fosse not only choreographed but danced with wife and muse Gwen Verdon, the only time the two appeared together on film. Fosse then went back to Broadway where he continued to choreograph many hit musicals and eventually got to direct. (His only other film performance was as

Figure 5.10 Bob Fosse and Tommy Rall in *My Sister Eileen* (1955, Columbia)

"the snake" in Donen's *The Little Prince* [1974]). One of Fosse's successes as choreographer-director in New York was *Sweet Charity* (1966–1967) starring Verdon, which he filmed at Universal in 1969 with Shirley MacLaine. Arriving as the hard-ticket musical had begun to bottom out, this expensive adaptation did not earn a profit, although it had its admirers.

Of the five films that Fosse directed three are musicals, each one bearing his signature, as Linda Mizejewski describes it in *Cabaret* (1972), a "visual style that has become synonymous with Fosse: dynamic editing, dazzlingly original and sexy musical performances, the use of suggestive and unusual lighting, and a camera that, during musical numbers, is almost as mobile as the performers" (Mizejewski 1992: 203). While *Cabaret* is considered his finest achievement, his third musical, *All That Jazz* (1979), is his most personal film and possibly the purist example of auturist cinema in the musical genre's history since Fosse cowrote the screenplay as well as choreographed and directed.

In *All That Jazz* Fosse unashamedly draws on his biography for the storyline of Joe Gideon (Roy Scheider), who is directing a new Broadway show starring his ex-wife, Audrey Paris (Leland Palmer), much as Fosse had directed Verdon in their final stage collaboration, *Chicago* (1975–1977), while at night he is editing a film about a comedian, much as Fosse had at the same time been editing *Lenny* (1974), about Lenny Bruce. Additionally, Fosse's former lover after separating from Verdon, Ann Reinking, plays Joe's lover, Kate Jagger, and many dancers from his Broadway shows and his assistants play those same roles here too. As happened to Fosse in real-life, the pill-popping, womanizing Joe has a heart attack, bringing the musical play's rehearsals and the editing to a halt, but unlike in real life, since Fosse returned to rehearsals of *Chicago* several months later, in *All That Jazz* Joe does not survive.

In the fantasy frame of *All That Jazz* Joe sits with a woman in white (Jessica Lange), her costume and wide-brimmed hat resembling that of a Ziegfeld showgirl, who turns out to be the Angel of Death, Angelique. Alone with him in what looks like a dressing room filled with mementos of his showbusiness career, Angelique asks questions that he answers. Her presence dramatizes Joe's self-destructiveness while providing exposition (Joe's background as a teenage dancer in the seedy world of burlesque entertainment) and characterization (his cheating on his wife and girlfriend, his drinking, his addiction to speed, his zeal for working). Many writers criticized this device for being too obvious and heavy-handed since the opening shots—a closeup of his eye receiving drops, Alka Seltzer fizzing in a glass, a bottle of Dexedrine—does much of that more economically.

What is interesting about *All That Jazz* is its wholesale deconstruction of show business, which actually reflects Fosse's ambivalence. For while the film's numbers express his cynicism, in tune with the treatment of the many show-biz types whom Joe works with, the same numbers also register the irresistibility for Fosse as well as Joe of pulling off show-stopping numbers. "To be on the wire is life," Joe exclaims to Angelique, and indeed, he seems alive only when working. His extended conversations with his former wife and daughter occur while he works out a number with each.

In the opening audience sequence, done to George Benson's "On Broadway," Fosse's camera is restless, traveling up, down, onstage, in the wings, in the seats, overhead, catching the dancers in odd angles or en masse as Joe moves among them, scrutinizing their auditions, sending most away. *All That Jazz* then records the travails of inspiration as Joe struggles to come up with an idea of how to stage "Take Off with Us": we see the composer demonstrating it for the producers and creative team, then Joe rehearsing it, and finally a tryout of his staging of the song, which as "Air-otica" morphs into an erotic tangle of bodies in multiple configurations and orientations. Later, to cheer up Joe, Kate and his daughter Michelle (Erzsebet Foldi) dance to Peter Allen's "Everything Old Is New Again," echoing Judy Garland's comparable number, "Somewhere at Last" in *A Star Is Born* (1954). In these numbers Fosse's editing, even more than his choreography, which reiterates many elements of his style already evident and "branded" on stage as his, captures the visceral appeal of dance.

Fosse reserves the full razzle-dazzle effect of musicals for the latter part of *All That Jazz*; these occur as fantasies of Joe as he goes under the knife and then as he dies. In the first long sequence, as from his hospital bed Joe watches himself film the numbers, the three women in his life each sing to him in high vaudeville style, the lyrics now reminding him of his abuses and hinting at what he will lose: "After You're Gone" (Audrey), "There'll Be Some Changes Made" (Kate), and "Some of these Days" (Michelle). A bevy of "old friends," showgirls dressed head to toe in white, surround Joe's hospital bed with their feathered fans as they serenade him with "Who's Sorry Now?" This sequence pivots between the numbers' entertainment value and the morbid context of Joe's delirium which produces them as his fantasy. In the second long sequence, as he is dying, Joe fantasizes being the guest subject on O'Connor Flood's (Ben Vereen) talk show with a live audience, which sends Joe off in grand and insincere style to "Bye Bye Love." As Winkler describes this sequence, despite the overwrought staging, "The cheering and stomping and crying are everything Joe could wish for. He has created the greatest show business ending of all time" (Winkler 2018: 243). However, silence follows the end of this fantasy as Joe's corpse is zipped into a body bag. Then as the screen goes dark, in what seems a raspberry to showbusiness, on the soundtrack Ethel Merman sings its unofficial anthem, "There's No Business Like Show Business."

Fosse's editing style in his three musicals works against creating the illusion of our watching a live performance from third-row center, which had been the convention of filming most numbers during the studio era. Fosse's influence on filming numbers with quick cuts that fracture a singular viewpoint in space has since been considerable and wide-ranging, evident in scores of music videos as well as contemporary musicals like Baz Luhrmann's *Moulin Rouge!* (2001) and Rob Marshall's *Chicago* (2002). Yet unlike the frantic editing by those two directors in their films, Fosse's never seems fearful of losing an

audience's attention; furthermore, he never loses sight of the performance as a whole performance despite his mediation, as happens with
Lurhrmann's and Marshall's treatments of numbers.

CABARET (1972)

Fosse is the only person to receive a Tony (for *Pippin*, 1972–1977),
an Emmy (for *Liza with a Z*, 1972), and an Oscar (for *Cabaret*,
1972) in the same calendar year, a record yet to be matched
with no contenders in sight. While *Sweet Charity* anticipated elements of the Fosse cinematic style with its emphasis on editing
numbers to capture the immediacy of dancing in flashes, iso-
lating quick glimpses of faces, torsos, arms, and legs as opposed
to showcasing the dancer's full body in long takes, *Cabaret* showed
this style more fully, with elements that became identified with
"Fosse" as a brand.

Before the "Mein Herr" show number begins in *Cabaret*, for
instance, Fosse cuts between Joel Grey, the emcee of the Kit Kat
Klub, and Liza Minnelli, who plays Sally Bowles. Shown backstage, she repeats the emcee's bawdy introduction as she pulls up
her stockings and fastens them with garters, the camera catching
her from behind and the side. After her introduction, she enters
the stage, struts around the emcee and begins the number; the
camera cuts from shots of Sally, for moments concealed by torsos
of ensemble members, getting into position on a chair, to a shot
of the chorus girls on her left, then a shot of those on her right,
then the full ensemble in a long shot as Sally begins to sing.
Fosse uses multiple edits to punctuate the movement of Sally and
the ensemble since for the most part they all remain on chairs,
standing on them, sitting down, kneeling, walking around them,
leaning on their backs or lying on the seats. Only in the final part
does Sally leave her chair to stride around the stage.

Figure 5.11 Liza Minnelli sings "Mein Herr" in *Cabaret* (1972, Allied Artists and ABC)

Kevin Winkler calls "Mein Herr" "the ne plus ultra of Fosse film numbers" because of the shots comprising it, which capture the dancers' "off-kilter body language," often photographs Minnelli "off to the side of the screen or framed between the dancers' legs and arms," as Fosse's camera moves all over the space, even at times positioned above in the fly space over the stage, at one or two other times venturing into the audience as waiters obstruct a view of the stage. As opposed to the dancing in his stage musicals, on film Fosse "can direct the audience's attention to just the detail he wishes it to see," catching a dancer "as she points up, down, or sideways on a specific lyric." In this way Fosse's camera becomes a partner in the choreography rather than a bystander recording the dancing in a handful of shots to showcase the performers. "Through quick cuts and razor-sharp edits, [this style of cutting] creates the visceral excitement of a live performance" (Winkler 2018: 149). The editing, in short, matches the rhythm of the fast-paced performance of Minnelli and her dancers, which is also to say that Fosse's editing seems like it is dancing.

Cabaret is considered a landmark musical for its distinctive editing, its gritty visuals, its casting of women in the Kit Kat Klub chorus who are "not quite young and not quite pretty, but who give off a heated sexuality" (Winkler 2018: 147), and the self-reflexive way it deconstructs the show musical and the genre's utopian sensibility. Although it is not clear whose idea it was to overhaul the stage source, the film plays against the comfortable conventions of Hollywood musicals for here the numbers evince a strong dystopian spirit and sense of professional, sexual, and ideological desperation. More important, Fosse integrates show numbers into his narrative without sacrificing their aggregate aesthetic.

On Broadway, *Cabaret* (1966–1969) was a book musical with the emcee and Kit Kat Klub numbers counterpointing and commenting indirectly on the action and with many other numbers occurring outside of the cabaret. The source material for *Cabaret* had a history in print and on stage and film prior to being musicalized. Christopher Isherwood's *Berlin Stories* (1945), consists of earlier novellas and stories, *Mr. Norris Changes Trains* (1935) and *Good-Bye to Berlin* (1939); the latter includes as its centerpiece a long story, "Sally Bowles." John Van Druten turned some of Isherwood's stories into a play, *I Am a Camera* (1951–1952), which was then filmed in 1955 with Julie Harris playing Sally in both versions. *I Am a Camera* basically featured two of Isherwood's plots, one revolving around Sally and a fictionalized substitute for the camera-like eye of his effaced narrator, who is a surrogate of the author, and another involving two young Jewish lovers. For *Cabaret* on stage, those Jewish characters were dropped and in their place was put an older couple, the Christian land-lady, played by Lotte Lenya, and a Jewish tenant, a grocer played by Jack Gilford. Although they become engaged, she breaks up with him as the Nazi violence against Jews mounts and she fears for her own survival. All versions retain the Sally Bowles figure but each adaptation had trouble inventing more than a cardboard character for the Isherwood substitute, primarily due to anxiety about representing the character as a gay man like the stories' author.

Fosse's film, which was shot in West Germany with many German performers and craftspeople, takes place in Berlin in 1931 (a year later than the stage musical's setting); the play's older couple was replaced by the younger one from Van Druten's version; and the Isherwood character, American and heterosexual on Broadway, was made British and bisexual, and Sally, British on Broadway, became American. Even more important, the book numbers were jettisoned. With two exceptions ("Tomorrow Belongs to Me," which turns into a Nazi youth anthem, and the older couple's "Marriage," which is now sung in German on a record), the numbers all happen in the Kit Kat Klub, where audience members are costumed and made up to resemble figures in German Expressionist paintings from the 1920s such as Otto Dix's portrait of Sylvia van Harden. This change focuses more attention on the show numbers' function as sidebar commentary while establishing the cabaret as a hot-house of vulgar entertainment and all sorts of sexual pleasures, in contrast with the mounting political and social turbulence and anti-Semitism occurring outside in the streets of Berlin, until Nazi Germany invades the cabaret and becomes incorporated into the final show numbers.

The framing of the musical with the Emcee's "Wilkommen" in the opening and in the closing moments makes this transformation very clear. Behind the opening titles we see shapes that turn out to be reflections in an overhead mottled mirror of the audience whose chattering we have been hearing, until the distorted, grinning face of the emcee appears; then we see his real face alongside his mirrored image as he begins to sing. The diegetic audience of the cabaret in the opening is distinctly bourgeois. Moreover, the Emcee's welcome is intercut with the arrival in Berlin of Brian Roberts (Michael York), the newly invented Isherwood surrogate. As the Emcee sings "welcome" in three languages to the cabaret audience, the editing implies he also welcomes Brian, who does eventually find his way to the club as a spectator. Via the cuts, the singing and music carries over into the daylight world of the German capital, indicating that, the lyrics to "Wilkommen" notwithstanding, the Kit Kat Klub and the city are not separate worlds but will both be overrun by history, already evident in the posters one may notice in the background as Brian travels through the city. In the finale, after the Emcee sings the brief reprise and disappears behind the curtain, the camera moves along the width of the stage to show the audience reflected in the overhead mirror; while the woman resembling the mannish von Hardon is still there, we cannot help but notice that one man after another in the crowd is a brownshirt with a Nazi armband.

The Emcee's numbers themselves trace the growing Nazification of Germany in 1931. At first the club prohibits Nazis from entering; as a man, presumably the owner or manager, is beaten in the streets, Fosse keeps cutting back to the Emcee and the Kit Kat Klub girls performing a Bavarian folk dance; they slap each other's knees as he mock slaps the women in their faces, paralleling the real beatings the man receives. At the end of the number, the dancers fall to the floor and the Emcee throws his hat into the crowd and crows with exaggerated delight, while the next image is the beaten, bloody man lying in the street. In "Money, Money," the dancing of Sally and the Emcee implies that sex is currency but the song verifies that the lack of real currency is the motive of their desire, mocking the hungry people outside while ignoring the Nazis' rise, evident in intercut shots of bloody bodies on the street. Likewise, in the "Tiller Girls" number, the female dancers and the Emcee in drag do a kick line across the stage. This number is intercut with the Nazi's attack on the Jewish family's house, including the murder of their small dog. Back on stage, the dancers turn around their bowler hats to look like helmets, place the tips of their canes on a shoulder, and goose step across the stage as the audience laughs raucously and applauds.

The confinement of numbers to the cabaret ties Sally to the Emcee's amorality since they are the only two main characters in the film with numbers and they perform one together; furthermore, Sally belongs to both the outside world and the club, indicating their underlying connections through sex, violence, and self-deception. Yet as a self-reflexive shading on their characters, Liza Minnelli is the daughter of film star Judy Garland and director Vincente Minnelli and Joel Grey the son of Jewish comedian Mickey Katz, and their familial backgrounds bring an aura of show-business history to *Cabaret* that their numbers similarly overturn by playing against those associations.

Of these two show-business children Minnelli's star text is the one complicated by Fosse since at times her numbers ("Maybe This Time," "Cabaret") are performed as showstoppers, evoking memories of her famous mother and meant to wow the moviegoing audience, while they express Sally's naivete and gullibility given the conditions of Berlin in 1931, yet at other times ("Mein Herr," "Money, Money") they reverse that innocent persona, indicating how Sally's identity as a divinely decadent femme fatale, with her Louise Brooks haircut, is a performance of sexuality from the movies and not a convincing one at that. The ambivalent treatment of Sally results from how Fosse uses editing to enhance his star's performance, his own history in staging showstoppers in hit Broadway musicals, and the cynicism of his later Broadway shows and *All That Jazz*, which is already in evidence in *Cabaret*.

"Cabaret" is definitely a showstopper; Fosse knows how this kind of number powerfully ends a musical, as happens with Barbra Streisand's "My Man" at the end of *Funny Girl* (1968). But how Fosse films, edits, and contextualizes "Cabaret" differs. When Liza Minnelli sings the title song at the end of *Cabaret*, the many cuts resist featuring her directly addressing the moviegoing audience, violating the longtime convention by which solos were shot. Fosse frequently shows Minnelli in profile; even direct closeups of her face has her looking up to the side with a hopeful expression as she sings. The numerous cuts indicate that the performance was shot multiple times with the camera positioned at different angles so the editing resists the impression that Minnelli's performance has been captured "live" even with lip-synching—except that Minnelli's gaze always indicates that she looks at the diegetic audience in the Kit Kat Klub, which surrounds the stage on three sides, much as, due to the editing, we are in effect watching her from different seats in the house. The times she looks more directly at the camera occur in a long shot that shows the entire stage and the backs of the audience watching her. Minnelli's voice sutures the entire number, to be sure, but Fosse's editing enhances the performance as can only happen in cinema, creating an effect of energy and movement that propels what is otherwise a performance happening in a very confined space.

But mitigating Minnelli's bravura star turn and Sally's optimism despite the fact that she has recently had an abortion and sent Brian back to Britain, immediately afterward we see the Emcee's face and the brownshirts watching her, implying that Sally will inevitably be engulfed in what will soon happen to Germany. Sally thus personifies the utopian spirit of the musical genre—hence her upward gaze while singing that she will hopefully and happily die from "too much pills and liquor" like her friend Elsie—yet, like the Emcee's, her performances at the Kit Kat Klub make just as vivid the genre's dystopian underside. Sally at times complements but at other times counterpoints the Emcee, matching his degeneracy with her innocence and his cynicism toward his audience with her need to be loved by hers. *Cabaret* itself keeps pivoting around these two extreme views; for while Fosse's staging of the numbers fully exploits the tawdriness and grotesquerie of the Kit Kat Klub on and off the stage, the numbers are still thrilling to watch.

6

EPILOGUE
LA LA LAND

La La Land (2016) has a relatively simple narrative. Mia (Emma Stone) and Seb (Ryan Gosling) meet cute, as do so many arguing couples when they first encounter each other in musicals; eventually they warm to each other, fall in love and share their dreams. Mia, working as a barista on the Warner Bros. lot, wants to be an actress; after failing to get parts, she writes and acts in a one-woman play as a showcase for her talent, but few industry people attend. Feeling she will not succeed, she and Seb quarrel and she leaves LA for her hometown in Nevada. Seb is a musical purist who sabotages the pianist job he has because he refuses to play the banal standards his boss orders; he wants to open a jazz club that will preserve the music's purity. In the film's conclusion occurring some time later, the couple has realized their professional dreams—he has his club and she is a film star—but their romance is over. Mia is happily married to someone else and has a child. She and her husband happen upon Seb's jazz club and go inside to hear the music. Embedded in this epilogue is a seven-and-a-half-minute fantasy musical sequence that, in a dance montage restaging the entire final section of *La La Land*, imagines a happy ending for Mia and Seb. In the final moments, however, Mia nods to Seb her acknowledgment of his success and leaves the club with her husband.

La La Land opened to nearly rapturous praise after premiering at multiple film festivals globally in the fall of 2016, followed by rave reviews and big grosses when it started its commercial runs in December, after which it swept many guild awards in Hollywood. With fourteen nominations, it was expected to dominate that year's Academy Awards but, after an infamous snafu in which it was wrongly announced at first, it failed to win Best Picture and ended up garnering only six awards, including ones for director Damien Chazelle and actress Emma Stone. Moreover, the film's critical and popular success yielded a backlash, with some complaining that Stone's and Gosling's voices were too weak to anchor a musical, their dancing too amateurish and untrained; some complaining that the film was too derivative in looking backward to be a reinvention of the genre; and some complaining about the whiteness of Chazelle's representation of Los Angeles—and of jazz. The one major black character, played by contemporary musician, songwriter, and record producer John Legend, sells out by going commercial (and when Seb goes on tour with his band to make some money, his traveling as well as that choice starts the break-up with Mia), in contrast with the ambition of Seb, a white man, to save the purity of jazz.

A fair assessment of *La La Land* falls somewhere in between the rapture and the condemnation. To start with, *La La Land* is very knowing about the generic history that preceded it, starting with the bright, bold color scheme that calls to mind the vividly saturated palette of studio-era Technicolor musicals. Chazelle builds explicit allusions to many classic musicals. Mia and her roommates' street number, "Someone in the Crowd," evokes "There's Gotta Be Something Better Than This" from *Sweet Charity* (1969), in which Shirley MacLaine, Chita Rivera, and Paula Kelly dance on a rooftop. Mia and Seb's challenge tap dance in "A Lovely Light" echoes Fred Astaire and Ginger Rogers's challenge dancing, their means of testing each other and discovering their parity, in "Isn't It a Lovely Day" in *Top Hat* (1935). The couple's dancing as they soar to the stars in "Planetarium," their friendship turning romantic, echoes numbers in which Astaire or Gene Kelly dances with Rita Hayworth or Cyd Charisse, enacting their mutual sexual enchantment as a couple. The fantasy montage in the epilogue quotes from *An American in Paris* (1951), *Singin' in the Rain* (1952), and *Funny Face* (1957) as Mia goes to Paris for her star-making role and this time Seb follows her there. And her discovering the jazz club by accident resonates with the final scene of *The Umbrellas of Cherbourg* (1964), Jacques Demy's French homage to the musical, when that film's two former lovers happen to meet again, each married to someone else.

The self-reflexivity of *La La Land* indicates how Chazelle consciously builds his film's organizing logic out of a tension between the utopian spirit of musicals and a dystopian sense of the ordinary world in which professional aspirations are antagonistic to romance and professionalism easily becomes careerism. For Chazelle also recognizes the split formal logic of Herbert Ross's *Pennies from Heaven* (1981) and Lars von Trier's *Dancer in the Dark* (2000), each of which treats its musical numbers as utopian fantasy and its melodramatic narrative as dystopian reality, the dominant condition of the characters' lives. That Mia and Seb achieve their dreams but at the cost of their relationship reverses how in classical musicals the professional plot and romance plot coincide. In backstage musicals the show hinges on the fate of the couple just as the couple's fate depends on that of the show—a maxim that the epilogue's fantasy ballet respects but which the epilogue itself abandons. For most of *La La Land* Mia and Seb are professionally stuck, their personal lives at a standstill until they fall in love; only in their numbers do they experience a sense of being liberated. *La La Land* recognizes the utopian pleasures of a musical—and of Seb and Mia's inhabiting one—while the epilogue's framing of its revisionist fantasy registers how experiencing that utopia fully is impossible for it can be rendered only as a musical, which the epilogue maintains is a Hollywood fabrication.

Stone's and Gosling's numbers work toward this goal, too, for they render Mia and Seb as ordinary people whose big dreams are out of their reach until musical numbers give such dreaming expression, form, and substance. But in contrast with Astaire and Rogers, say, Mia and Seb do not emerge as larger than life through their singing and dancing, thus inviting a different means of viewer engagement, one based more in straightforward identification than in the awe and wonderment one experiences when watching that older star couple dance. This is why some viewers were able to duplicate rather exactly Stone and Gosling's dancing to "A Lovely Night" in YouTube videos whereas few could do the same for Astaire and Rogers despite the merchandising of printed instructions in the 1930s that encouraged fans to try. For all the romantic sheen and glossy look of *La La Land*, this is to say, Chazelle readjusts what can make star performances like Stone's and Gosling's so affecting in a twenty-first-century musical.

Admittedly, here a white couple still has the most freedom to sing and dance in the street, as Richard Dyer has observed of older musicals (Dyer 2002: 41). That may still be the price of making a big-budget mainstream musical in Hollywood today. Gosling and Stone are box-office names and had already starred opposite each other in two previous films. Chazelle's first independent film, *Guy and Madeline on a Park Bench* (2009), which began as his student project while at Harvard University and, in its plot and numbers, can be seen as a trial-run for *La La Land*, featured an African American male and a Latina female in the lead roles. The opening number of *La La Land* is therefore critical in setting up how to view what follows.

This multiracial, multiethnic opening, in which traffic stops and one by one everyone on the freeway leaves their cars or vans to sing and dance joyously to "Another Day of Sun," establishes both the anomie of life in Los Angeles, where people like Mia and Seb spend so much of their day in their cars, and how, more than simply offering escapism or glitter and tinsel, "the musical allows characters to shift from a state of isolation to one of inclusion. It creates a sense of belonging for both its characters and its audience in the process." Desirée Garcia points out that this opening number implicitly connects the two leads of *La La Land* to characters in older ethnic musicals made outside Hollywood. "Ministering to audiences who were dealing with the

Figure 6.1 "Another Day of Sun" in *La La Land* (2016, Summit and Lionsgate)

pains and anxieties of migration, ethnic musicals offered stories about people who burst into song as a way of establishing connections to one another and to their homeland" (Garcia 2017).

No number in *La La Land* tops the thrill of watching this bravura opening. It is telling that Mia and Seb do not participate in "Another Day of Sun" or that their own numbers never approximate its choreographic intricacy or full sense of a vital, energetic, interactive singing and dancing community. That this opening reminds us of the liberation, of connection even more than escape, that musicals have always imagined calls attention to how, through the greater intimacy of Seb and Mia's numbers, but also through Gosling and Stone's skillful acting, *La La Land* scales down the opening's utopian ethos of inclusion until the fantasy sequence in the epilogue. Then the fantasy sequence, the equivalent in *La Land Land* of the ballet in *An American in Paris*, offers the satisfying resolution that the narrative itself denies, which is also to say that the fantasy sequence recognizes and welcomes the Hollywood artifice that enables a musical. When all is said and done, this may be how *La La Land* reinvents the musical genre for a millennial sensibility— if the genre ever needs to be reinvented. For whether in terms of its being praised or critiqued, what *La La Land* made evident in 2016 is that the Hollywood musical continues to mean something important for audiences.

WORKS CITED

Altman, Rick (1989) *The American Film Musical*, Bloomington: Indiana University Press.

Altman, Rick (2010) "From Homosocial to Heterosexual: The Musical's Two Projects," in *The Sound of Musicals*, Steven Cohan (ed), London: British Film Institute and Palgrave Macmillan: 19–29.

Arbuthnot, Lucie, and Gail Seneca (2002) "Pre-Text and Text in *Gentlemen Prefer Blondes*," in *Hollywood Musicals: The Film Reader*, Steven Cohan (ed), London: Routledge: 77–86.

Basinger, Janine (1993) *A Woman's View: How Hollywood Spoke to Women, 1930–1969*, Hanover, NH: Wesleyan University Press.

Brueggemann, Tom (2018) "'Mamma Mia! Here We Go Again': 3 Reasons Why Musicals Are Box Office Gold Again," IndieWire (20 July), www.indiewire.com/2018/07/mamma-mia-here-we-go-again-musicals-box-office-1201984961/. Accessed 20 July 2018.

Burlingame, Jon (2018) "'Baby Driver' Director, Crew Prepped to the 'Millisecond' Before Production Began," *Variety* (22 February), https://variety.com/2018/awards/baby-driver-steered-by-choreography-1202707188/. Accessed 23 February 2018.

Cohan, Steven (1999) "Queering the Deal: On the Road with Hope and Crosby," in *Out Takes: Film and Queer Theory*, Ellis Hanson (ed), Chapel Hill, NC: Duke University Press: 23–45.

Cohan, Steven (2005) *Incongruous Entertainment: Camp, Cultural Value, and the MGM Musical*, Durham, NC: Duke University Press.

Cohan, Steven (2017a), "The Manic Bodies of Danny Kaye," *Cinema Journal*, 56, no. 3: 1–23.

Cohan, Steven (2017b) "The Musical Comedian: Bob Hope in the *Road to* Series and *Son of Paleface*," in *Stars of Hollywood Musicals*, Marguerite Chabrol and Pierre Olivier Toulza (eds), Dijon: Les Presses du Réel: 143–151.

Decker, Todd (2011) *Music Makes Me: Fred Astaire and Jazz*, Berkeley: University of California Press.

Doty, Alexander (2000) *Flaming Classics: Queering the Film Canon*, London: Routledge.

Dyer, Richard (2002) *Only Entertainment*, 2nd edition, London: Routledge.

Dyer, Richard (2004) *Heavenly Bodies: Film Stars and Society*, 2nd edition, London: Routledge.

Dyer, Richard (2012) *In the Space of a Song: The Uses of Song in Film*, London: Routledge.

Farmer, Brett (2000) *Spectacular Passions: Cinema, Fantasy, Gay Male Spectatorship*, Durham, NC: Duke University Press.

Feuer, Jane (1993) *The Hollywood Musical*, 2nd edition, Bloomington: Indiana University Press.

Fleeger, Jennifer (2014) *Sounding American: Hollywood, Opera, and Jazz*, New York: Oxford University Press.

Fordin, Hugh (1984) *The Movies' Greatest Musicals: Produced in the USA by the Freed Unit*, New York: Frederick Ungar.

Garcia, Desirée J. (2014) *The Migration of Musical Film: From Ethnic Margins to American Mainstream*, New Brunswick, NJ: Rutgers University Press.

Garcia, Desirée (2017) "*La La Land*'s Debt to Ethnic Musicals of Yore," Zócalo Public Square (14 February), www.zocalopublicsquare.org/2017/02/14/la-la-lands-debt-ethnic-musicals-yore/ideas/nexus. Accessed 16 May 2018.

Glenn, Joshua (1997) "Camp: An Introduction," *Hermenaut* 11–12 (winter): 2–21.

Grant, Barry Keith (2012) *The Hollywood Film Musical*, Malden, MA: Wiley-Blackwell.

Griffin, Sean (2002) "The Gang's All Here: Generic versus Racial Integration in the 1940s Musical," *Cinema Journal* 42 (fall): 21–45.

Griffin, Sean (2018) *Free and Easy? A Defining History of the American Film Musical Genre*, Hoboken, NJ: Wiley Blackwell.

Guittar, Stephanie G., and Nicholas A. Guittar (2015) "Intersectionality," in *International Encyclopedia of the Social & Behavioral Sciences*, 2nd edition, volume 12, Amsterdam: Elsevier: 657–662.

Harvey, Stephen (1973) "Interview with Stanley Donen," *Film Comment* 9, no. 4 (July–Aug), 4–9.

Knight, Arthur (2002) *Disintegrating the Musical: Black Performance and American Musical Film*, Durham, NC: Duke University Press.

Knox, Donald (1973) *The Magic Factory: How MGM Made* An American in Paris, New York: Praeger.

Mast, Gerald (1987) *Can't Help Singin': The American Musical on Stage and Screen*, Woodstock, NY: Overlook Press.

McBride, Joseph (2018) *How Did Lubitsch Do It?* New York: Columbia University Press.

McCracken, Allison (2015) *Real Men Don't Sing: Crooning in American Culture*, Durham, NC: Duke University Press.

McLean, Adrienne (2005) *Being Rita Hayworth: Labor, Identity, and Hollywood Stardom*, New Brunswick, NJ: Rutgers University Press.

McNally, Karen (2010) "Sailors and Kissing Bandits: The Challenging Spectacle of Frank Sinatra at MGM," in *The Sound of Musicals*, Steven Cohan (ed), London: British Film Institute and Palgrave Macmillan: 93–103.

Mizejewski, Linda (1992) *Divine Decadence: Fascism, Female Spectacle, and the Makings of Sally Bowles*, Princeton, NJ: Princeton University Press.

Morris, Jan (1987) *Manhattan '45*, New York: Oxford University Press.

Newton, Esther (1979) *Mother Camp: Female Impersonators in America*, Chicago: University of Chicago Press.

Ovalle, Priscilla Peña (2011) *Dance and the Hollywood Latina: Race, Sex, and Stardom*, New Brunswick, NJ: Rutgers University Press.

Pullen, Kirsten (2014) *Like a Natural Woman: Spectacular Female Performance in Classic Hollywood*, New Brunswick, NJ: Rutgers University Press.

Rogin, Michael (1996) *Blackface, White Noise: Jewish Immigrants in the Hollywood Melting Pot*, Berkeley: University of California Press.

Rubin, Martin (1993) *Showstoppers: Busby Berkeley and the Tradition of Spectacle*, New York: Columbia University Press.

Smith, Susan (2005) *The Musical: Race, Gender and Performance*, London: Wallflower.

Trenholm, Richard (2018) "Inside the Oscar-Nominated Sound That Steers 'Baby Driver,'" C-net (2 March), www.cnet.com/news/inside-the-oscar-nominated-sound-that-steers-baby-driver-julian-slater/. Accessed 17 December 2018.

Vogel, Shane (2008) "'Stormy Weather': Ethel Waters, Lena Horne, Katherine Dunham," *South Central Review*, 25, no. 1: 93–113.

Williams, Alan (1981) "The Musical Film and Recorded Popular Music," in *Genre: The Musical*, Rick Altman (ed), London: Routledge and Kegan Paul: 147–158.

Winkler, Kevin (2018) *Big Deal: Bob Fosse and Dance in the American Musical*, New York: Oxford University Press.

SELECTED FURTHER READING

Babington, Bruce, and Peter William Evans (1985) *Blue Skies, Silver Linings: Aspects of the Hollywood Musical*, Manchester: Manchester University Press.

Barrios, Richard (1995) *A Song in the Dark: The Birth of the Musical Film*, New York: Oxford University Press.

Barrios, Richard (2014) *Dangerous Rhythm: Why Movie Musicals Matter*, New York: Oxford University Press.

Cohan, Steven, ed. (2002) *Hollywood Musicals, The Film Reader*, London: Routledge.

Cohan, Steven, ed. (2010) *The Sound of Musicals*, London: British Film Institute and Palgrave Macmillan.

Croce, Arlene (1972) *The Fred Astaire & Ginger Rogers Book*, New York: Galahad Books.

Delamater, Jerome (1981) *Dance in the Hollywood Musical*, Ann Arbor: UMI Research Press.

Genné, Beth (2018) *Dance Me a Song: Astaire, Balanchine, Kelly, and the American Film Musical*, New York: Oxford University Press.

Harvey, Stephen (1989) *Directed by Vincente Minnelli*, New York: Museum of Modern Art and Harper & Row.

Hirschhorn, Clive (1991) *The Hollywood Musical*, revised edition, New York: Portland House.

Kennedy, Matthew (2014) *Roadshow: The Fall of Film Musicals in the 1960s*, New York: Oxford University Press.

Kessler, Kelly (2010) *Destabilizing the Hollywood Musical: Music, Masculinity and Mayhem*, London: Palgrave Macmillan.

McElhaney, Joe, ed. (2009) *Vincente Minnelli: The Art of Entertainment*, Detroit: Wayne State University Press.

McNally, Karen (2008) *When Frankie Went to Hollywood: Frank Sinatra and American Male Identity*, Urbana: University of Illinois Press.

Mueller, John (1985) *Astaire Dancing: The Musical Films*, New York: Knopf.

Shearer, Martha (2016) *New York City and the Hollywood Musical: Dancing in the Streets*, London: Palgrave Macmillan.

INDEX